*To Mal
with a
grateful appreciation for
our partnership in ministry*

Walking Home

Simon Harvey

This book is based on the blog written during my walk:
http://simonwalkshome.blogspot.com

For Jennifer

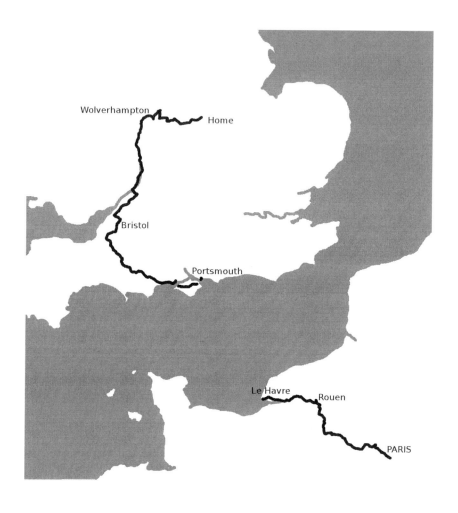

The route of my long walk home - a 535 mile pilgrimage, in a roundabout way

Contents

Acknowledgements

Without a large number of very special people, this whole adventure would not have been possible.

I am grateful to The Right Revd Tim Stevens, Bishop of Leicester, for permitting me a sabbatical break and for the personal interest he took in my walk.

Many thanks to The Revd Canon Dr Mike Harrison, for his wisdom and the encouragement to see the potential in a sabbatical for renewal as well as rest, and to The Revd Dr Stuart Burns for his support.

I am hugely grateful to The Revd Canon Michael Rusk, The Revd Paskal Clement, Dr Hugh James, Colin Chettle, Anita Chettle and Paul Webster for the additional workload that they carried during my absence from the parish. It is wonderful to work in a team of such capable clergy and lay ministers.

I appreciated the way Malcolm Britton, The Revd Richard Curtis, Margaret Gillespie and Claire Stapleton took such care of Reader Ministry work in the diocese while I was away.

I greatly valued generous sponsorship from Ecclesiastical, specialist insurers of churches, whose bursary scheme allows many clergy to travel or study during sabbatical breaks from ministry.

The people of the Parish of Oadby, in particular members of St Paul's Church, were remarkably generous and supportive. Since 2003 we have walked together in an adventure with God and I shall always treasure our partnership. *I thank my God every time I remember you, constantly praying with joy in every one of my prayers for all of you, because of your sharing in the gospel.* (Philippians 1.3-5.)

Many thanks to Vivien James, for checking this manuscript.

I enjoyed amazing hospitality from friends and family along the way and delighted to meet up with you all. Thank you all so much - for the comfortable beds, the dinners and breakfasts and most of all, for your company.

Most of all, I want to thank my amazing family - Jennifer, Jon and Phil. Thank you for allowing me to disappear for a while and for being there when I returned. I love you more than I can say and am proud of you all.

I met Vera for the first and last time while she lay dying in Leicester's Royal Infirmary. As I walked up to her bed at the end of the ward, she smiled. We had been praying for her in church and her daughter told me that the end of her life was very close. All words seem inadequate for these situations. I have learned from dying people that it really is alright not to have anything profound to say.

"How are you feeling?"

She closed her eyes and through smiling lips said, "I'm going home!"

I thought I knew just what she was thinking. In case I had got it wrong, I asked, "How do you mean?"

Vera's eyes opened wide and she raised her head from the pillow. "I'm going home to be with Jesus!"

Introduction

It was good to sit on a plain stone bench and to sip cold water in the underground subway before summoning the energy to surface again to an unseasonably hot Paris. This was my first resting spot, a chance to collect my thoughts while I enjoyed filling my lungs with air that was much cooler than the streets above. I looked at the holidaymakers and sightseers around me. Our itineraries were so different. This, I realised, was when my status changed. I was no longer a tourist. I had become something else - a walker, a wanderer, a pilgrim.

I was on my own now, *properly* on my own. Jennifer had walked with me the first two miles away from Notre Dame Cathedral. It was an enjoyably slow, lingering walk with much unsaid. We smiled with tears in our eyes and then we hugged and kissed and held and finally let go. We began our longest separation for at least twenty eight years, perhaps even the longest since we'd met at the age of twelve. As she crossed the Solférino footbridge, I kept walking along the embankment of the Rive Droite, looking over my shoulder every few moments to catch her looking back. We waved and walked on.

At times, the Champs Élysées had been so busy I had to nudge through the crowded pavements with a "Pardon!" or "Excusez-moi!" My bulky gear didn't help. I hadn't thought that I would be the only one wearing a rucksack, reckoning that it's a popular city on the backpackers tour. Yet everyone else, it seemed, was chic and refined. The clientèle at the boutiques and jewellers were obviously well-heeled. But so were the young people who chatted outside McDonald's. During my practice walks from home every Monday morning I had looked a bit of a berk - dressed in my Tilley hat, walking shirt and trousers, boots and backpack. In Oadby's quiet residential streets I had grown accustomed to withering looks, promising myself that it would be different during my big adventure. I should have realised that on this Day One I was even more out-of-place. Nor did I know that in all sorts of ways, this out-of-place feeling, this dis-location and sense of being foreign was going to intensify in the coming weeks, rather than disappear. "Don't you know that I've just started a seven week walk over five hundred miles long?" I felt like shouting. No, that would have convinced them: "He really is a berk."

The subway under the Arc de Triomphe allows visitors to ascend to the top of the arch, which would otherwise be marooned in the very centre of the Étoile, the star-like junction of twelve roads. I hear that car insurers treat all accidents here on a knock-for-knock principle, so drivers take their chance as they hurtle into the ten-abreast stream.

Only for a moment did I think about paying the fee to ride the lift to the top of the arch. It would have given me a glorious view but I decided that I needed to get on with the day's journey, a seven-mile route to Nanterre. To be a tourist can sometimes feel like a sheep, following the flock, ticking off the must-see attractions. Being so close to the tourist honey-pot and choosing not to look, *that's* independence, that's being a traveller.

The subway tunnel that led away to the west from the bottom of the lift shaft was much quieter than the one that I had walked along from the east. I had already reached the limits of tourist Paris. Now I was walking among the locals. Like some of them, I was on my way home.

Napoleon's vision for the Arc de Triomphe was that his victorious armies would return to Paris by marching under it after their glorious conquest and subjugation of the enemies of the Second Empire. His troops would enter the outskirts of the nation's capital and follow the Avenue de la Grande-Armée, with the victory arch and cheering crowds before them. It occurred to me as I walked the other way that the orientation of the whole route was perfect for the homecoming of an army returning from the Channel ports. In other words, this was a route conveniently designed for the rejoicing of a French victory over the British. Napoleon's defeat at the Battle of Waterloo put paid to that, of course. I smirked inwardly. Reversing Napoleon's plans, I was walking under his homecoming arch at the outset of my homeward-bound pilgrimage.

The Avenue de la Grande-Armée is now home to numerous scooter and motorbike dealerships, which equip Parisians with their beloved two-wheeled transport. All across the city, at all hours of the day and night, the streets are full of bikes. Wiry youths twist open their throttles well before the traffic lights turn green and scream away across the cobbles with petite girlfriends lazily balanced on their pillion seats.

At one point I had thought about doing an epic motorcycle journey as the focus for my thirteen-week sabbatical. But a bike as big as my 750cc Suzuki carries me a long way in a day and frankly, a round the globe trip felt just a little beyond my organisational ability. Pushing myself beyond familiar limits was something I wanted to do though. I had even wondered about a long ride on a cheap scooter, just for the fun of it. Several people have even used the ubiquitous Honda C50 Cub step-through scooter to do a circumnavigation so I wouldn't be breaking new ground by pootling around Europe on one. Besides, I realised the novelty of zinging along at thirty miles per hour would wear off pretty quickly. My motorcycling days are well behind me now, in any case. This trip, among many other things, was going to be about a slower pace, the discovery of a new form of transportation for me - walking.

I'm not a walker, and never have been. The non-disabled, non-pushchair parking space that is closest to the supermarket door and available is the one I go for. Walking has been the way I reach my real transport - the car, bus, or train.

I have realised for a long time that more walking would be good for me but I scarcely leave myself enough time between appointments in my busy parish ministry. I'm always checking the clock to see if I can fit in one more phone call or email before heading off to another meeting or pastoral visit. Then I realise I've left it too late, which I hate, and take the car instead. When I've walked between local appointments I have even felt guilty. Guilty that I could have squeezed more real work in instead of indulging myself with something so slow. Now though, without the pressure to be productive or efficient, I was learning that I *can* go slowly. Walking was part of what this indulgently *un*-productive sabbatical was about. Walking for fitness and health, walking for the sheer challenge of it, walking in order to pray and think, walking as the simplest way of going home.

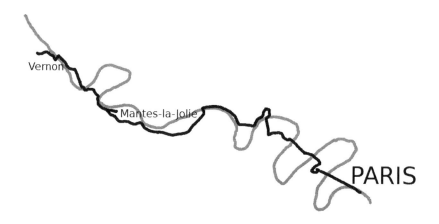

Paris to Vernon - 66 miles, never far from the meandering River Seine

Chapter One - Paris to Vernon

Jennifer and I were talking about the possibilities for my sabbatical a year before it began. The Dean of Leicester Cathedral had conducted my 'Ministry Review', asking all sorts of questions to lead me through a reflection about my role. I enjoyed the process, since the work and life of a vicar is something that still feels like a huge privilege and stimulated challenge. When I suggested that it would be good timing for me to have a sabbatical in 2009 she happily agreed. My friend Mike, our Director of Mission and Ministry in the Diocese, was very supportive too and the bishop said yes. I think this is what they mean by "getting all one's ducks in a row". I was all set and keen.

Clergy sabbaticals are taken for one of two reasons, either because vicars are exhausted, run down or depressed or more positively, because they are looking for refreshing challenges, opportunities for study or reflection. I felt that I was in this second and more positive category. I loved the idea of a sabbatical as *renewal leave* - a chance to step back from a role which is full-on and demanding, to gain a broader perspective on who I am, where I'm going and how best I can serve God through the church in the world. That sounds a bit grand and, to be frank, it's not the way I answered people on the footpaths when they asked me what I was doing there. Most conversations went a bit like this:

"Morning!"

"Morning!"

"Beautiful/dreadful day isn't it?"

"Yes, I know - lovely!/horrible!"

"Are you walking far?"

"About five hundred miles, actually!"

"*Really?* How long is that taking you?"

"Seven and a half weeks. Fifty-two days, to be exact."

"How do you get the time off work?"

"I'm a vicar. We're encouraged to take a three-month sabbatical break every ten years or so. This is my first."

"You jammy so-and-so!" (Well okay, they usually said "Oh!" but I could tell that's what they were thinking.)

The look I received was often a doubtful one. That's likely to be because I had just delivered a lot of information in a few words but it might be because I usually looked dog-rough, not dog-collared. Announcing that I'm a vicar is sometimes a bit of a conversation-stopper and most people widen their eyes and give a nervous grunt, especially if we've been talking for a while before my identity surfaces. I think they probably mentally back-track on our conversation, trying to remember if they've said something offensive. (Most people seem to think that clergy are so easily shocked that even the mildest of comments would appal us.) Guilt is another explanation. Sometimes when I reveal my occupation, I immediately receive all sorts of explanations about why someone doesn't go to church any more or how they used to sing in a church choir or how they always go to midnight mass at

Christmas. I smile and nod - I really am more interested in them than their church-going record.

To be honest (I promise to try to be honest in this book) in explaining my presence on the highways and byways and my absence from the pulpit I guess *I* feel just a little bit guilty too. The world of work, for most people, is a world of insufficient resources, over-supervision and impossibly high expectations. Spending fourteen years in engineering management makes me very aware that in my current 'job' I now have enormous freedom and flexibility. Being a vicar is demanding, difficult and sometimes overwhelming. But I don't have the dismal challenge of slogging away unproductively in a dead-end occupation with little reward. I really love what I do.

And now I had three months off. A sabbatical in which to explore, do new things, rest and play. What a privilege!

As Jennifer and I thought about what I could do with the opportunity, we knew it made sense for me to go away for a long time. As I say, I love what I do and I find myself more fulfilled, peaceful and happy when I'm working than when I have time off to myself. Of course, proper family time is fantastic and we always enjoy our holidays as well as having regular fun together. But if I were to stay at home, I would run the risk of doing much of what I normally do. It would also be hard to be in hiding, as it were. How could I not engage with parishioners and church members?

But I asked myself if I could really leave Jennifer for so long. And what about Jon and Phil, who would be approaching AS and A2 exams in the sixth-form? Was this all selfish indulgence, or could we find a way of making it work for all of us?

I had mentioned to Jennifer how I fancied doing a long walk. Another sabbatical idea was to re-visit the Barton Hill district of Bristol, in which I had worked and studied urban theology in the late 1990s. At that time it was a tough, disadvantaged neighbourhood and had just received a huge grant for a major regeneration programme, the *New Deal for Communities*. The ten-year programme had recently ended and I thought I could do some research into what had changed and to see if and how the church had contributed. In thinking this through, I soon realised that what could be more significant in this would be to understand how much *I* had changed in the decade. That's when the core of the plan came together.

Walking between places and people which have been special to me would give me plenty to reflect on. It would help me remember where I had been and to understand where I'm going now. The slower pace of walking would be helpful, liberating me from my routines, getting me fitter. It also had theological potential - my mind raced with verses from the Bible about walking. I remembered how Gerard Hughes' book, *In Search of a Way* had helped me when I first thought seriously about Christian faith in my mid-twenties. He undertook a walking pilgrimage to Rome and described the way that the outer journey on the road related to an inner spiritual journey with God. Perhaps I could do something similar.

"Why don't you walk home?", asked Jennifer one evening.

"That's it!" I said. "I don't want to walk away from you, from all this. If I walk home, I'll be always walking towards you."

I lay awake in bed that night, thinking about where I could walk, where to begin and how I could join up significant places and people in a way that led back to Leicestershire.

By the time Jennifer had come home from work the next day, I had both a plan and a dream. My plan involved a basic route through Bournemouth (where our good friends Jenny and Chas live), Bristol (where we lived for two years while I studied theology), the West Midlands (home to most of our wider family and where we lived and worked). The route would be around three hundred miles, not in a straight line but a crescent-shaped curve. My dream, however, was more ambitious.

"I've been thinking about this walk, darling." I began when we shared a morning cup of tea. "I want it to be the main focus of my three-month break, so how would you feel if I was away for... six weeks or so?"

To my surprise, Jennifer said she thought that would be great, despite the fact that we'd never spent more than five days apart in our twenty-three year marriage.

"I reckon walking from Bournemouth to Oadby would only take me a month. What if I began in Paris? We could have a mini-second-honeymoon." I ventured. This sealed it, the dream became the plan. I was going to be Walking Home.

Our three days in Paris began a week after Easter. I had taken a week after my last duties in church to make final preparations. We took the train from Leicester to St Pancras Station in London, which was conveniently also the new terminus of the Eurostar service for Paris. Our journey from home to hotel in Paris took us just seven hours.

On the way south, Jennifer and I talked a lot about where life had taken us since we began our marriage in Paris. In 1986, a young electronics engineer and his administrative assistant wife had also taken the train to Paris but back then it had involved a ferry crossing from Dover to Calais and taken a whole day. Everything was different now - Jennifer, me, our marriage and the journey - but still the same. We celebrated the ways that we have grown, but always in relation to each other, like climbing plants that find support and space in their growth together.

As the Eurostar picked up speed on the French side of the Channel, I calculated it was travelling about fifty times faster than I could walk. Fields and towns flashed past the window. Each minute the train was covering almost an hour's worth of my long walk home. From the time I drank the first sip of a coffee to the moment I finished the cup, the train had covered the same distance that I would manage in half a week. I gulped.

Our room in the *Hotel Suede St Germain* was comfortable and the location superb. We didn't need a taxi or the *Metro* to reach a restaurant near the *Tour Montparnasse*, which we'd decided to ascend for a midnight view of the city. After dinner, we found our way to the entrance of the tower, paid the charge to a bored attendant and were flung by Europe's fastest elevators to the fifty-sixth floor in thirty-seven ear-popping seconds.

In 2008, the skyscraper was voted the second ugliest building in the world by a group of travel editors; apparently only the *Boston City Hall* in Massachusetts is less attractive. I felt that the judgement was a bit harsh but admittedly it is a bit of a brutal and unsympathetic building. It has the great problem of standing in a city of architectural loveliness. I'm sure that if it could be relocated to, say, Leicester's city centre, it wouldn't be so bad. The redeeming feature of the dark grey monolith is that its observation decks offer some of the best views in Paris. (Some say that they are the best views in the city precisely because you can't see the *Tour Montparnasse*.)

The bar on the fifty-sixth floor looked like it hadn't been improved since the day the tower was opened in 1972. It reminded me of a set from the children's science fiction puppet series, *Thunderbirds*. Perhaps it was the schmaltzy music that was being played, or the bored bar staff wearing fixed expressions, or the chocolate brown décor. After a quick look around we headed back to the stairwell and climbed four more flights to reach the roof itself. I have stood on the flat roof of a block of flats only once and there is something exhilarating about it, even in the midst of a poor housing estate. In Paris at midnight, it was altogether inspiring. It felt like we were on a platform, held high to the night sky. In the warm darkness, the stars were eclipsed by circling airliners and most spectacularly, by the Eiffel Tower, which spun a searchlight from its summit into the night.

We were caught in the intense white beam and watched it scan across the city and suburbs, dimming and brightening again until its flash filled our eyes once more and made everything else dark for a moment. It was magical.

There were only three or four people on the roof when we arrived and by eleven thirty, Jennifer and I were alone. It felt like the city was ours. We walked the perimeter of the roof, in the dusty westerly breeze. At midnight, just as we were getting used to the beauty of it all, the Eiffel Tower sparkled with thousands of flashing xenon lights. We were spellbound.

We spent much of the second day of our break in the Musée D'Orsay, a museum of art and sculpture in a wonderfully renovated railway station. The building itself was impressive enough but we were thrilled by the impressionist and other nineteenth-century paintings.

We enjoyed the works of Monet, Gaugin, Pissaro, Toulouse-Lautrec, Renoir, Cezanne, Signac, Degas and many others. I recognised some of the most famous paintings, including one or two which we bought as prints and put up in our little Wolverhampton home when they were fashionable in the late nineteen eighties. But there were many surprises too. I loved the joy and exuberance of Renoir's *Bal du Moulin de la Galette*, full of youthful fun. By contrast, the woman in Degas' *Au café du l'Absinthe* looked pitifully sad in contemplation of her life. Caillebotte's *Raboteurs de Parquet*, depicted men hard at work stripping the floors of an apartment.

It seemed to me that a significant element of impressionism is its everyday subject matter. Who would have thought that a group of floor strippers would make subjects for a fabulous painting? I relished these celebrations of the ordinary and anticipated that my walk would take me through a huge variety of scenes of everyday life. The goal of my pilgrimage wasn't going to be some exotic shrine but home. As I walked, would I be able to see things through an artist's eyes, cherishing familiar people and ordinary places, as jars of clay holding extraordinary treasure?

–

I woke after a sleep disturbed by excitement. This was Day One, the twenty third of April, 2009. I was about to start the biggest adventure of my life.

Outside Notre Dame Cathedral, right in the heart of Paris, a small brass plaque has been set in the pavement. It is literally overlooked by hundreds of visitors each day but for Jennifer and me it had special significance. The plaque marks *Kilometre Zero*, the spot from which all distances in France are calculated. It's scarcely bigger than a dinner plate, with a simple compass rose at the centre and the inscription, *"Point zero de routes de France"* around its circumference. Jennifer took a picture of my first stride and I tried to think of something memorable to say. I managed, "Here we go, then."

We crossed the bridge and walked together along the embankment past the Louvre and the Tuileries Gardens. After our parting on the *Right Bank* of the Seine, Jennifer and I went our separate ways. I took the Champs Élysées to Arc de Triomphe and then the Avenue de la Grande-Armée up to Porte Maillot on the Périphérique, Paris' inner ring road. By now I needed a loo-break, so headed into the *Palais de Congrés* conference centre. It was pretty quiet but once again I felt conspicuously dressed among the suited business people. Boldness, I remembered from my days of site-visits as a young engineer, gets you a long way in an unfamiliar building. Look like you know what you're doing and you can get practically anywhere.

Another subway took me under the busy ring road and I surfaced in Neuilly-sur-Seine, a wealthy neighbourhood, in which French President Nicolas Sarkozy was mayor for nine years. I was expecting something like Mayfair or Belgravia but didn't see signs of anything especially posh, except for the little lap dogs carried by one or two stylish ladies, and luxury cars.

I kept walking and headed towards the skyscrapers of La Défense, the business district which competes with Canary Wharf and Manhattan. By now the towers were looming large and I could make out some of the famous logos from the big companies. At ground level, the road disappeared and pedestrians walked along vast piazzas, with huge expanses of textured concrete. I couldn't think of anywhere in Britain that felt the same, except for those nineteen sixties university campuses that are not much loved these days.

La Défense's grand squares and broad walkways are on a scale which is anything but human. The giant towers are, I assume, designed to be admired from a long distance and their effect on the solitary walker who walks past them is a little intimidating. There were only a few people around and it was hard to see what the vision for the place might have been. In the quieter areas it felt bare, even bleak.

The *Grande Arche* is an amazing construction, created to mark the western end of the historic axis of monuments along the alignment from the Louvre at the east, via the obelisk at Concorde and the Arc de Triomphe. It has the feel of a vast temple and is approached on an ever-ascending route. Even within its own structure it has hundreds of steps, each wider than any I've ever seen. Climbing them it seemed that the architects wanted to suggest to mere walking mortals that their ascent was for some cultic purpose. But there was no ceremony or altar waiting for me at the top of the steps, just a ticket booth offering a ride in an elevator. I declined and felt inwardly pleased with myself for refusing another altar-call.

A cityscape designed to spring architectural surprises is hard to navigate on foot and I got lost as I tried to leave Defense. I thought I was heading in the right direction when I walked the entire length of a wooden pier, only to find that it led nowhere and I had to backtrack to awkward steps and ramps. I had visions of designers plotting "playful" spaces and cursed their Gallic creativity.

Eventually I discovered the way out into Nanterre, whose tower blocks were of the depressing-residential rather than glamorous-corporate variety. I started to feel uncomfortably on-edge, anxious for the first time about being an alien and worried that my peculiar appearance might attract hostility rather than plain disparagement.

The blocks in Nanterre were strangely painted in a kind of camouflage, with swirls of tope and khaki. It was the kind of concrete development which lends a probably undeserved menace to the bored youths hanging out on the streets. Most, if not all, of this was in my head. No one spoke to me, let alone intimidated me. But nonetheless I was aware of being an outsider, an intruder even, on someone else's turf. I kept checking the map to confirm I was on the right route, not worrying if this indicated I was from out-of-town (the red rucksack had surely already signalled that to anyone within a mile of me).

I thought how odd it was that I felt concerned to remain on my chosen path, as if that legitimated my presence or made me any safer. I was, after all, simply going for a stroll but on an epic scale. What was I going to do if I was challenged? Hold up a map and say, "It's alright! Look, I planned to be here"?

As I walked among some of the toughest-looking residents, a car waited at a red light next to me, engine revving. The windows were open and loud music boomed out from within. A motorbike raced up to the car, its rider made his gloved right hand into the shape of a handgun and pushed it through the open window into the car driver's face.

"Police!" the rider shouted. Then he roared off, laughing.

I wasn't sure if the tough guys in the car took it as a joke, which is what I assume it was meant to be. It struck me that the idea of a police officer pushing a gun into a car was probably not too far-fetched, otherwise the gag wouldn't have worked.

Eventually I found the *Hotel d'Amandier*, one of the most expensive on my whole trip, though the price did include both dinner and breakfast. I was disappointed with my Spartan room but relieved to have found sanctuary in a fierce neighbourhood. The restaurant was surprisingly good, with friendly staff and a customer with a dog-in-a-bag, which he fed with titbits from his plate. Ornamental dogs, I had noticed, were a feature of Paris. i saw many more dogs being carried around in their purpose designed carry bags. Some are even toted in slings, like newborn babies.

Back in the hotel bedroom I returned to my walking verse for the day. I had looked up plenty of Bible verses which relate to walking and thought it would be a good idea to keep a verse in mind each day of my long pilgrimage. So I had chosen a verse for each day of the walk, taken in the order that they appear in the Bible, writing down the reference in a little *Moleskine* notebook and copying out the text of the verse from the Bible on my mobile phone at the start of each day. Of course, reading the Bible in a sentence at a time isn't the best way to discover its message of hope and meaning. Simply trusting that a couple of dozen words picked at random might have something relevant to the moment isn't always going to work. Yet it was fascinating how surprisingly helpful these walking verses turned out to be. Quite often during the walk I found myself turning them over in my mind. They led me to unplanned meditations, especially in quieter places where my imagination could run along ahead of me, like a little child on a family holiday stroll, feeling the freedom to explore the world in the company of its loving Father.

I wondered how to include these short verses in this written account of my journey and even whether I should do so at all. They had featured in my daily blog entries but quite often I felt that the hastily-written reflections that I made each day could not do anything like justice to them. As a reader, you may be keen to know more about the verses and frustrated that I am going to be so brief. Or you may be nervous of having scriptures quoted and fear that I'm going to preach to you. Throughout this book, I shall try really hard not to betray your trust in either way but please be forgiving when as you walk with me, I might occasionally tread on your toes. It's a hazard of keeping company with a walker.

So instead of pretending that the Bible isn't a "lamp for my feet and a light to my path" (as the writer of Psalm 119 described the word of God) or attempting a weighty exegesis, I'm going to risk a paragraph or two for each day.

I began in the book of beginnings, in Genesis 13.17: *Rise up, walk through the length and the breadth of the land, for I will give it to you.* I thought that perhaps I shared with Abraham, to whom God spoke, in the promise of new discoveries and of making an adventure of life. This walk was for me, just like Abraham, a gift to be received.

At the end of Day One I had walked eight miles and enjoyed knowing that the following day I had be enjoying my first rural miles, with a peaceful walk through forests and fields. That's not how it worked out.

—

Day Two was due to be the first proper day's walk, and at twelve miles, around the average for the whole route. I had booked all the accommodation for the journey several months in advance, so I knew each day where I was heading. I had used the internet to reserve all the hotels in France, as my French isn't good enough to be sure that I would get telephone bookings right. This limited me to chain hotels and created a lot of work in order to plan a walk-able route but at least it gave me the security of knowing that I had somewhere to sleep each night. I was working my way out to the coastal port of Le Havre at the mouth of the River Seine, where I would take the ferry to Portsmouth. However, as the Seine meanders in huge sweeping bends, I would be making regular hops across the higher ground that it cut through to traverse Normandy.

It made sense to keep the walking distance for each day to a manageable amount. I planned to build up to a pattern of six days walking with a rest day on Sunday, knowing that I had to get fitter as I walked. So the first part of the walk included a period of acclimatising and an element of toughening-up. It was all, to one extent or another, an act of faith. The complicated itinerary I had worked out during many winter nights at home in Oadby was transcribed from computer spreadsheet into my Moleskine notebook. I kept a spare copy printed on waterproof paper in the secret pocket of my Tilley hat.

After praying and writing and a good breakfast of croissants, jam and coffee, I knew that I was heading for a *Formule 1* hotel in Conflans-Sainte-Honorine. I had printed maps on waterproof paper but wanted to keep my options open as to the precise route, depending on how I felt each day.

Having said that, the options for Day Two were not terribly varied. I was happy enough. Following the previous evening's walk among the tower blocks, I was keen to ensure that I didn't accidentally stray too far into the toughest of Paris' *banlieues*. Some of the eastern suburbs were ravaged by riots and unrest in 2005 and 2007 and their residents often feel themselves to be living in hopeless exclusion in a France that regards them more as unwanted guests than as citizens of the Republic. I have an interest and a concern for the inner-city and a lot of experience of living in mixed communities so I was curious to see what awaited me in France, but also a little apprehensive. Most of all, I was acutely aware of being a stranger, an alien myself.

Looking at my maps again, I realised that because the excellent 1:25,000 IGN series showed residential buildings in black, it was easy to see the geometric patterns of the tower blocks. The organisational urbanism of Le Corbusier's architecture and those that followed him, left Paris with suburban high-rise buildings that had a recognisable foot-print. I felt a little guilty at making some judgement about my safety on these streets from information as sketchy as the shapes of buildings but decided that these were early days and it was best to be cautious.

The sun was already shining brightly as I walked north through the university district, where I could hear the rumble and clatter of construction work going on all around. I turned onto a bustling busy road which carried me across the Seine at Pont de Bezons. Bezons is an outer suburb of Paris and showed as much of the segregation as I have seen elsewhere in France during many holidays. There were crowds out shopping but I saw few white faces - most people appeared to be of north African descent and again I realised that I stood out with my absurd walking gear on urban streets and my lily skin. I didn't feel scared so much as alert, noticing that I had developed a habit of warily scanning my surroundings as soon as I turned each corner. Perhaps, I thought, these are primitive instincts that surface for the lone walker in a strange land. How far should I trust them to keep me safe, or would they keep me suspicious and unable to engage with people?

I thought about the Algerians and Moroccans and their families, what it might be like to walk in their shoes. In some ways this wasn't their land either. I understood that they are often made to feel as though they do not really belong here. Across the world millions of economic migrants and refugees try to find their way in a new country, without the luxury of a credit card and maps like me, let alone my multi-pocketed hiking trousers and round-the-world underpants. These lives before me seemed as far removed from the Parisian west-end as mine did. Were they also planning to make their way home at some point, or was this home?

I had planned a picnic in the Foret Domaniale de St-Germain-en-Laye later in the afternoon, so bought a slice of pizza from a down-market boulangerie. I wondered if it would survive the heat of the day in the top compartment of my rucksack. The temperatures were soaring now. But the thought of sitting in the shade of a tranquil forest and even napping in the afternoon was a good one to hold in my mind. I could not have guessed then just how differently things would work out that day.

The town of Houilles is twinned with Surrey's affluent Chesham and, sure enough, there was quite a change of scene. Now only white faces, on quieter streets with detached houses. Walking a significant distance through urban areas makes me wonder why the change between affluent and deprived neighbourhoods is so abrupt. It was clear that the people of Bezons and Houilles kept to their own towns and I assumed that the residents of one had little idea of how their near neighbours lived. Yet there were no checkpoints or walls between the two. These clear demarcations exist only in 'social mind' of unspoken shared understanding and the subtleties of property prices. Yet they're so powerful. Why don't we mix more than we do?

Crossing the tracks again, this time literally, I headed into Sartrouville, a town with no discernable centre or attraction. The Seine, which I had crossed an hour earlier, returned to my route after looping its way on a long meander. On the far bank a splendid château came into view across the river.

I crossed the Seine again and entered Maisons-Laffitte, which proclaimed itself to be "The City of the Horse." Alongside the river, shaded by willows, its racecourse enjoys a wonderful setting and the Château itself houses the national racehorse museum.

This was more like it. I felt at ease and a couple of hours of walking had relaxed me. I was in no rush but checking the map, I could see that I had two options for getting beyond the Château. The western route would take me along the main road again, but had the advantage of bringing me more quickly into the forest. The eastern route would mean picking my way through quieter residential roads. After dithering for a moment I plumped for the right.

I wasn't far in to the rather affluent-looking housing estate when I saw a sign, *"Église Anglican"*. Within minutes I found Holy Trinity Church, whose noticeboards were all in English. One still displayed the notice for its Annual Parochial Church Meeting and I thought about the APCM meeting at Oadby which had taken place the previous evening. Every Church of England parish holds such a meeting, during which elections take place for the various roles. These meetings are sometimes dismissed for being too formal and stodgy but at their best these are places to hear about developments in the life and mission of the church and to plan for the future. This was the first year in the twenty-three since I had become a Christian and began to belong to a church that I had not attended an annual meeting.

Before the sabbatical began, I wondered how I had handle the fact of not being involved in the life of St Paul's and the wider parish of Oadby. I noticed that being reminded of the annual meeting left me peaceful and at ease, for which I was immensely thankful. After all, God was in charge and there were plenty of gifted and responsible people in the parish to make the decisions that are necessary.

Having come this far, I reckoned it might have been a nice idea to call on the vicar and to say hello. I might even get a cup of tea, I thought. The address of his vicarage was displayed on the noticeboard. I found the house and rang the bell. Getting no answer, I stood on tiptoes to peer over the high fence. It all appeared quiet. As I crossed the road again, two gentlemen approached me and asked me what I was doing. I explained that I was looking for the priest, in very poor French. I made hopeful supplementary gestures. Not knowing of an international sign for "priest" I drew a clerical collar around my neck with pinched fingers several times. It didn't seem to help.

We got talking though. Helmut spoke reasonably good English and I persisted with my broken French, to ensure Jean wasn't left out of the conversation altogether.

It turned out that the door that I had called at was not the vicar's door, but Helmut's. He had seen me taking an interest in his house. He told me that he initially thought I was a burglar, then realised I didn't really look like the sort to break in to his home. He also told me that he was worried by my frantic gesturing. He could understand what I was saying but my mimed clerical collar looked to him like a menacing cutting of the throat. He thought I was trying to tell him that the priest had died!

Helmut and Jean invited me to walk into town with them, where they were going for a drink. I gladly accepted and was thankful for their generosity and interest in what I was doing. The fact that I was a priest seemed to them to be both reassuring and curious.

"But walking?" asked Helmut, "Why don't you ride a bicycle?"

I realised that in France this was going to be the obvious question for many hundreds of kilometres ahead.

Helmut and Jean were concerned most of all about my safety, especially about my planned walk through the forest in the afternoon. They shook their heads. "You mustn't go", Helmut said, "it's very dangerous!"

I was puzzled. It looked perfectly blissful on the map.

"There are many..." Helmut's sentenced tailed off. He looked as though he had thought of a word but was hesitant to use in front of a man of the cloth.

"...*transvestites!*"

I coughed and laughed. "No!"

But he was serious. "Some of them are vicious. They will

steal your money and attack you!"

"Really?" This was about as much as I could manage in reply. This announcement was the last thing I expected and frankly I wondered if Helmut and Jean were leading lives that were too sheltered in their quiet suburb. It couldn't be as bad as that, surely? But it was.

We drank pastis at the appropriately named *Café Anglais*, talking gladly of Helmut's work as an inventor and sadly of Jean's terminal illness. Helmut whispered that Jean gets depressed and that he likes to take him out at least once a week. I spoke of my work as a "protestant priest" and they were surprised to hear that I had a family. Both assured me that they believed in God but that they never went to church, something I hear often enough. I promised to pray for Jean in the coming days and tears appeared in his eyes. It seemed like a small thing for me to offer and his profound and unarticulated gratitude surprised me.

My encounter with Helmut and Jean was both wonderful and unsettling. I had been greeted first with suspicion and then with hospitality. It was looking as though on the French part of my walk, I was always going to be regarded as strange. But was Helmut's warning sensible advice, or the result of paranoia? I thought again about the way that I had already seen people keep to their own turf, dividing themselves from others into enclaves and ghettos. I would be crossing thousands of these subtle boundaries in the five hundred miles ahead of me. It made me feel like a kind of brave pioneer, proving to the locals by my intrepidness that the people in the next town or housing estate were really alright after all. I wanted Helmut and Jean to be wrong. I wanted to end the day laughing at their fearful isolation and rejoicing in my adventuring.

So I set off into the forest, adapting my route only slightly. My compromise with fear was to follow Helmut's advice and to stick to the main roads, rather than walk into the heart of the forest on footpaths. The new route added a couple of miles to my journey but if they were right about the threats that awaited me, I might be safer being visible to passing traffic, rather than miles from anyone.

I felt my heart begin to pound as I approached the forest on a quiet road, telling myself not to be silly, to breathe slowly and deeply. It took another dozen steps for my shoulders to tighten and my lungs to take nervous sipfulls of air again. After half an hour, at a small car park in a roadside clearing I found a log and sat down to eat my pizza, which had not taken the journey well. I picked off the furry green mould which had begun to grow on its crust, ate it hurriedly, then set off again. This was daft, I had only rested for a few minutes and now I was marching at a fast pace. "Slow down. Breathe. It's okay." I told myself. And I prayed.

The road through the forest was fairly non-descript. The traffic was quiet, with cars passing me every couple of minutes. I thought I saw the drivers eyeing me nervously but then told myself that this was nonsense.

Before long I noticed plastic bags tied to the trees alongside the roads at intervals. Occasionally, there was a parked car, pulled off the road and in the verge. A hundred metres ahead of me I saw a man walk from among the trees and into his car, then quickly leave. I guessed at what was happening.

I reckoned that the plastic bags in the branches were a kind of signal to passing drivers that sex, presumably for a price, was available in the trees. I approached the next bag dangling from a branch curious if I had guessed correctly. Sure enough, each bag indicated the presence of a prostitute. Glancing into the trees, I could see them, looking at me and assessing the likelihood of trade. I gulped.

I wondered how many of the cars which passed were driven

by 'punters' and I thought I had as much to fear from them as from the women, or men dressed as women, in the trees. The biggest risk, I realised, would probably come from the pimps who dropped the women off and who sometimes waited for them in their cars.

The women themselves (at least they all looked like women to me) were very obvious about what they were doing. It reminded me of one of those newer safari parks where visitors are encouraged to look among the foliage for exhibits. But here there were no information panels to tell me about their habits. I just had to work it out for myself, which was pretty straightforward. Some sat on logs, some even reclined among the bracken a few feet from the road, in enticing poses. Others preferred to stand farther back in the trees.

Drivers would sometimes slow at the sign of the plastic bags to take a look. I had hear them call out from their cars, presumably to ask a price or to check the details of the offer. Often they would then drive on to the next prostitute, which made me realise these transactions were not furtive and fast but that a real market was in operation.

I also realised that this was a drive-through arrangement, not a place for pedestrians. Gosh! I thought. Now I am scared. Keep going.

I reached another plastic bag and from the corner of my eye glimpsed a tall lady, standing about twenty yards from the road in the trees. I turned to look and as she saw me take interest she opened her jacket to reveal her bare chest. Oh gosh! I snapped my head back to the road in front of me and walked even faster.

I walked as quickly as I could, checking the map to make sure I was on the right route and calculating the distance to the edge of the forest. 1:25,000, that means an inch on the map is half a mile. I reckoned. That meant it would take two hours to cross. I checked again. I prayed. I prayed again, the kind of urgent and wholehearted praying that fear inspires. And I skipped through the forest like little red riding hood on performance-enhancing steroids.

At one point, my prayers were interrupted by a dreaded sound. A vehicle approaching from behind slowed down until it was alongside me. I carried on walking. The driver matched my pace and called out to me something that I couldn't understand.

Here we go, I thought. How was this going to end? Would my planned fifty-two day adventure end on the second day in a ditch in a forest with me robbed, beaten - or worse? A strange calm descended on me. The driver shouted again.

I recognised the word *cherche*. He was asking if I was looking for something. "Non!" I called back firmly, still walking.

Again he asked, this time looking agitated. I was more insistent, "NON!"

He looked angry and frustrated as he pulled away. Had I survived an encounter with a dangerous pimp? Or, as I considered in the following minutes, had I refused a generous offer of a lift from a man who recognised a stranger in need?

I thought again lots about this as I walked on, heart pounding. Helmut had initially suspected that I was up to no good, then worked out that I was harmless, if a little peculiar. First impressions can obviously be wrong but to what extent should I trust my instincts when safety is concerned? Was it sensible to distrust everyone, or was that the road to misery? These thoughts churned around my mind as I pushed on past more plastic bags, a grimy railway siding and onto the main N184 Route Nationale dual carriageway.

This was a fast road, with few places for motorists to stop. I thought that being so busy it would also make it much less likely for prostitutes to operate. Yet even here, I saw a couple of cars pull over, dropping women off. On the other side of the dual carriageway I saw two women get out of a car and enter the woods, one was no more than a teenager. It was a nasty business.

The main road brought me to the banks of the Seine once again for my third crossing of the river that day. There was a depressing moment when the "No Pedestrians" sign on the bridge made me think that I was stranded. The fast-pace running of the gauntlet in the woods had left me exhausted and I was desperate not to be lost. With great relief I found a footbridge and staggered into Conflans-Sainte-Honorine.

I had been holding Genesis 17.1 in my mind all day: *I am God almighty. Walk before me and be blameless. And I will establish my covenant with you.*

Again, God is talking with Abraham (technically, he is still Abram as this conversation begins). And again God assures him of his sovereignty and makes a promise. This time, though, there are two sides to the bargain. In response to the invitation Abraham is asked to walk in a blameless way. The Book of Genesis is raw and unashamed in its description of violence, exploitation, infidelity, rape and prostitution. In the midst of this darkness Abraham managed to walk straight paths, ignoring the seductive temptations that lay either side and any doubts that God would never leave him alone.

My feet were sore, having walked too fast for too long without a break. The fear had exhausted me too. I picked up supplies in the village and found the cheap hotel where I had a reservation.

The day had initially been planned as a leisurely twelve miles, much of it in the tranquillity of the trees. It turned out to be a strenuous and anxious 14.5 miles instead. I lay on the bed, found that I had blisters on the inside of both heels and thought about what might have been. If I been less exhausted, I might have had nightmares but I slept solidly for ten hours.

–

The *Formule 1* is the lowest rung of the ladder in the Accor Hotel group. We've used them while travelling across France to reach a family holiday destination and they have provided basic accommodation at low cost. But the fall of the pound against the Euro following the credit crunch of 2008/9 meant that I was getting poor value for money.

Whichever *Formule 1* hotel one stays in, the rooms are identical. This creates a disorientating déjà vu on every arrival and every waking up. To one side of the window is a sink and, on the other, a television set. A red tubular-frame fills one wall. At the base, this structure supports a double bed with a thin mattress and at the top, a single bunk bed. Even the room's only light is incorporated within one of the vertical tubes. Twisting the tube directs the light towards the bed or alternatively to the sink. You can't have both.

Down the corridor, a series of showers and WCs are automatically cleaned with high pressure jets every time an occupant leaves. The reception is staffed only at breakfast time and for a few hours in the evening.

Despite the grim regime, I was content with clean sheets and somewhere to wash. Breakfast was predictably basic. Poor coffee, orange squash, bread and jam. But I could eat as much as I wanted, so I piled my red plastic tray with as much calorie-charged carbohydrate as I thought I could manage to set me up for Day Three.

I had checked my feet again when I woke and found that the blisters had not subsided during the night. I am fortunate in generally not getting blisters and was rather surprised that they had appeared. The dash through the forest had definitely taken its toll. I had packed some *Compeed* blister pads and read the instructions about using them at the first sign of a stinging hot sensation. My feet were already well past that stage so I thought I had better give the blister pads a go.

Strangely, these weren't my only blisters. I had also lost skin from the tips of the first three fingers on each hand. It took me a while to work out that this strange injury was caused by repeated flicking of the seams of my trousers as I walked.

I'm not normally an eater of jam. At home, every year or so I buy a jar of some fancy conserve which is destined to go mouldy after just a couple of spoonfuls are consumed. But now the physical effort of walking was changing my appetite. Like an expectant mother whose body knows what it needs, I was developing cravings, becoming especially fond of sweet things, even though I rarely eat them at home.

Fuelled-up, I set about writing and uploading my thoughts to the blog which I was keeping to record the whole adventure. Each time I sent updates, I collected notifications of comments by friends and unknown readers. These felt like a real blessing at the start of the day. By the time I had prayed and packed, I didn't get away until 10:45am. Although I had a medium-length walk of about 13 miles ahead of me, this felt a bit late.

In Genesis 24.40, an unnamed servant of Abraham arrives at the end of a long walk and begins to explain the mission he's been sent on: *Abraham said to me, "The Lord before whom I walk will send his angel with you and make your way successful."*

I thought a lot about Abraham's servant during the day. His master had dispatched him on a special trip to a far away land, to find a bride for his son, Isaac. I imagine Abraham would have wanted to make the journey himself and choose a suitable girl, but by now he was infirm and unable to leave home. So bearing this enormous responsibility, Abraham's servant set off and arrived at the town of Aram-naharaim, where he found Rebekah drawing water.

The verse begins the servant's explanation to Rebekah's brother, Laban, about the purpose of his long trip. It reminded me of the curiosity of strangers about the reasons for my peculiar pilgrimage. I was also especially struck by the hospitable welcome which Laban gave the servant. The kindness of strangers is a precious thing to us wanderers.

The weather was changing. Cool, cloudy and wet air was pushing up from the south and the patches of blue were gone by lunchtime. I spent a good deal of the day wearing a jacket for the rain that never came.

I walked south to the rivers Oise and the Seine whose confluence gives Conflans its name. The mighty Seine was now twice as broad as it had been in Paris and its swollen waters had created large mid-stream islands. On several of these I saw gravel being extracted, then loaded into huge barges.

In Andrésy smells of mowing blew on the breeze. People were on the move, some cycling, some running, some sculling up the river, and some catching trains, perhaps for a Saturday's shopping in Paris. I thought about the high garden walls and the connections between privacy, wariness of strangers and suspicion. To me it felt that suburban France is more wary than the English Midlands. Perhaps that was simply because I am an "insider" in Oadby and not an alien.

At lunchtime I found a market on the banks of the Seine. I stocked up for lunch with apples, a heavy traditional loaf, and a small but powerful-tasting piece of goat's cheese. The place was bustling and joyfully cramped, making for a clumsy passage between the stalls with my rucksack.

I walked away from the river past Chanteloup Les Vignes, between the village and the dowdy apartment blocks of la Noë and Daurade. In a further exploration of how to look less like a foreigner, I reckoned that carrying my plastic shopping bag (in which I had hidden my hat) was an improvement. I also practised a casual nonchalance, as though I walked those roads every day.

Beneath the Pont aux Chevre in Triel-sur-Seine I sat to eat my lunch by the river, watching the barges as the clouds were thickening with rain that, as it turned out, never fell. A group of locals came out to sit on the next bench and I longed to be able to talk with them. I wasn't lonely in the way that I had expected. This was a kind of solitude in the midst of people; every ungreeted passer-by and every avoided eye contributing to an unusual kind of isolation.

From Triel, I took the long straight road through Vaux-sur-Seine, whose *Mairie* was made of charming coloured bricks, much more attractive than most small-town civic buildings back home.

The afternoon walk through Meulan was very quiet and I had the impression that France mostly naps after lunch on Saturdays. The pavements were broad but their coarse flinty gravel, presumably excavated from the Seine's islands, made for heavy going. It was like trudging on a shingle beach.

I deliberately slowed my pace, remembering that, in the old cliché, this was a marathon, not a sprint. Then I worked out that my walk was actually going to be more than twenty end-to-end marathons and the thought made me take a deep breath.

Going more slowly was definitely better for my legs and had none of the aches and pains in my knees and thighs that I first got when walking long distances in the last year. I paused regularly, taking advantage of the seats at bus stops to massage my calves and stretch.

It was fine to go slowly. Too often, we make a journey obsessively calculating how quickly we can reach our destination. I knew that I would spoil the walk if I was concerned about speed and I resolved to celebrate the days that worked out longer than expected. After all, what would an extra hour in a budget hotel room do for me?

Despite a slower pace, my blistered feet didn't seem to be improving. I took off my boots and socks during a rest break at a bus shelter. Perched on the seat I saw that the *Compeed* blister pads had begun to slide up my heels, despite their stickiness. The constant striding had pushed them up away from the blisters and their adhesive was beginning to bind to my socks. This wasn't going as planned. I switched to the alternative insoles that I had packed in a last minute decision before I left home. These felt better - at least I was putting pressure on a slightly different part of my feet now.

I eventually crossed the river once more at Les Mureaux, and found my way onto the tatty industrial estate where my even

tattier *Formule 1* hotel awaited. It was getting close to six o'clock when I checked in and I was too tired to complain about a room that was smelly and whose walls were filthy. Once I had checked that the bed linen was reasonably clean and after I threw off my rucksack, undone my boots and flung my sweaty socks to the floor I sank back into the mattress.

I had checked *Google Maps* on my phone and searched for a restaurant near the hotel. It turned out that a *Buffalo Grill* was practically next door and I laughed at the memory of holidays in France where long journeys were broken with a meal at these wild-west themed chain restaurants. Steak and chips washed down with a Kronenbourg 1664 was just what I needed. The staff were friendly and the meal very satisfying indeed. Back to the hotel room and I was getting used to my solitary lifestyle. It was great that I was able to pick up a mobile phone signal in every town and good to end the day by talking with Jennifer, Jon and Phil.

Adjusting to being alone had not been such a big shift for me, perhaps because I was so occupied with the walking. By now, the days were taking shape. A pattern was beginning to emerge of mornings where I felt alert, followed by a relaxed mid-day mood and a tired but not unhappy evening.

In the solitude, something else was happening - the walk had become all of me. I was losing perspective, not in an unwelcome way, but I found I had lost track of the overall route. Of course, I still knew where I was heading in subsequent days and weeks and I was still recording where I was in relation to the whole journey but all that was not in my immediate experience was somehow theoretical. More and more, I was living in the moment, not abstracted from the time and place that I occupied. As someone who constantly plans and prepares, this felt wonderful. It's just me and the moment and the road. I thought. This rare kind of mindfulness can liberate us from the hopes and fears that preoccupy a lot of the way we live, where the focus of our attention is somewhere other than where we physically are.

I watched the TV news bulletins describing a new 'flu outbreak which had emerged in Mexico, possibly from pigs, and again I slept for almost ten hours.

–

As early as Day Four, I changed my approach to daily route planning. I had thought that I might look at the map each day, work out where to buy lunch and dinner, where to rest and what to go and see. But it turned out that I had become much more relaxed about these things. As long as I had something to eat, I could let the day unfold itself to me on its own terms. I didn't need to work out anything - all would be well.

After another plain *Formule 1* breakfast, shared with some surly commercial travellers, I set off on the road from Les

Mureaux, towards Flins-sur-Seine. The first part of the walk took me through a small wood, the Bois-de-Saint-Vincent. My heart sank when I saw my first plastic bag tied to a branch. But it was tatty and had obviously been there a while. Besides, it was a Sunday morning. Surely, I hoped, it was not a prime time for prostitution. Thankfully, I saw no one.

I thought about those at home who would be gathering for church, especially when I heard the bells ring in Epône. Our little church bell would soon be signalling the start of worship at St Paul's in Oadby. There were more reminders of home. When I left, the blossom was coming out on the pavement trees in Launde Road. Here in Epône it was already gone from the branches and was blowing into piles along the kerbs.

The streets really were quiet and I got the impression that everyone was occupied with Sunday lunch, or already enjoying a long afternoon nap. In the morning there had been cyclists, riding in large *peletons* but I presumed they were now home enjoying a family Sunday. It reminded me of who I was missing and my two-apple lunch just wasn't the same as our normal Harvey family Sunday dinner.

The road towards Mantes-la-Ville was straight, broad and again, deathly quiet. Sycamore trees, pruned into precisely identical amounts of bushiness, lined the way. I walked on the lovely flat cycling piste alongside the carriageway and noticed that it was marked with the circular scourings of a road sweeping machine. It was spotlessly clean. In the UK, cycle lanes are often so poorly maintained they make for a miserable surface for walking, let alone cycling, with broken surfaces littered with rusting fragments of lorries and rubbish. It was odd then, that I saw only a couple of cyclists in an hour.

I passed the huge Renault factory, which I read about in a local paper the following day. Here the *Renault Clio* is built by a workforce of three and a half thousand. The company has committed itself to switching to an all electric vehicle production line by 2012. The French attitude to the global economic recession appears much more positive than the British in investment in manufacturing and construction. I had already seen news bulletins reporting on the massive scheme to extend Paris. This proposed a corridor of new industrial and commercial development all along the Seine to the coast. By contrast, the United Kingdom appeared to be focussed on rebuilding its credit-led economy.

Porcheville is home to a behemoth of a power station. I could see its twin chimneys during the previous day and they loomed during the whole of Day Four. It burns coal to produce an immense 2500 megawatts of electricity for the energy giant EDF. And how much carbon dioxide, I wondered.

Mantes-la-Ville was pleasant enough. I saw a sign indicating Commonwealth war graves on its cemetery entrance and popped in to take a look. This was the area where liberating armies of the western allies first crossed the Seine in August 1944 but I couldn't find any war graves, except for the large central memorial. The man unloading trays of flowers from the boot of his car for a family grave couldn't help either. I did notice one grave from 1971 in which three generations of a family of five appeared to have died in a single tragic accident of some sort.

A large cellophane factory provided employment in the town for many years but that has long since gone. Nowadays, the town makes saxophones and clarinets, and probably a little more besides.

The tower blocks and apartments en route to the *Formule 1* hotel were apparently largely occupied by Ghanaians, according to the community centre I passed. Here the quiet French Sunday changed dramatically. Lots of children played outside, not only in the playgrounds but also on the street. In the more affluent areas, children play only in their own gardens, I had noticed. I drew more curious stares but felt at ease.

It had been a relatively easy day, with only ten miles to cover. I arrived at the *Formule 1* hotel before four o'clock and enjoyed the anticipation of a long rest and to give my blistered feet some air. The hotel though, was even worse than the one I had begun the day in. There was a cigarette burn in my pillow case and I shared the shower with someone else's sticking plaster.

My walking verse for the day was Genesis 24.63: *Isaac went out in the evening to walk in the field and looking up, he saw camels coming.*

Well, I had seen no camels. The verse completes the story which I had begun the day before. Rebekah had returned with Abraham's servant and Isaac spotted their caravan of camels as they came back home.

The phrase "walking the fields" has held particular meaning for me for a while. I discovered somewhere a long time ago, that farmers walk their land, not only to enjoy it, but also to look for the unusual or the out of place. They might spot a broken fence, the first signs of some blight on the crops, or the state of drainage in the soil. They might also spot opportunities and decide to try a new variety on a certain field.

I've borrowed the term and applied it to my own work. For me, "walking the fields" is about a regular review of what's going on around me. Most days, I walk into the church, notice what's been left, remember the last service and the mood and insights we gained when the chairs were filled by a congregation at worship. I anticipate the next and remember who I need to call.

I am teased for being too interested in the details of church life. At least some of the time, I should really interfere less and allow others to get on with things more. One of the opportunities of a sabbatical is the chance to let go and to let others know that I am confident in their leadership while I am away.

–

Day Five was the last in my first sequence of back-to-back walks. In practising over a period of nine months I only had opportunity to go for a long walk on my regular day-off - Mondays. A three-day sequence of walks around Leicestershire a few weeks before I set off for France definitely helped to prepare me for the challenge I was now tackling but it was clear that by now I was tired. I had read Mark Moxon's excellent account of his Land's End to John O'Groats walk and noted how he got more tired over the first ten days but by the time he reached the two week point, he was getting fitter and stronger.

I was experiencing something similar, feeling more fatigued at the end of each day than the day before. I was looking forward to the first complete rest on Day Six.

My feet, though, were still sore. I gave up on the blister pads and pulled them off altogether. The skin was thin and sensitive in places and raw where the blisters had burst. The alternative insoles seemed to be helping, though they didn't give as much support to the arches of my feet. I risked, according to the podiatrist I had visited months before, painful shin splints. My health and fitness was always going to be a bit of an issue as I was not used to exercise or sport. I was basically happy with the way things were going, though the sore throat that I had picked up was slowly worsening.

Thanks to a navigational blunder that added an hour and a half of plodding, my last day before a break turned out to be tough. Even so, and despite a soaking, Day Five turned out to be the best so far.

I know exactly where I went wrong. It was the moment I

came out of a corner shop, clutching a can of pop and looking for somewhere to sit. I spotted a bench outside the *Mairie* in the dismal town of Rosny-sur-Seine and thought about how good it would feel to take off my boots.

I had satisfied my newly acquired taste for sugar with a can of tropical fizzy drink, so perhaps it was the sugar-rush that made me set off again in completely the wrong direction. I had really enjoyed getting into the walk. The pain of blistered feet had eased after a few miles. After being on the road for a couple of hours, everything seemed to be ticking along nicely.

The woods next to the road were marked out with a path for recreational walking and running and there were occasional signs next to various kinds of apparatus. I ignored their injunctions to jump, stretch, lunge and squat. Nor did I fancy the balance-beams and chin-up bars. The path was parallel to the road and made for an easy route. Only after I puzzled over an advertising billboard for a restaurant in Mantes, where I began the day's journey, did I realise that things had gone wrong.

I checked the map and realised that I had almost reached Le Val-Fourré, the "world's largest housing project", according to the Wikipedia online encyclopedia that I read later in the day.

I am normally pretty good at knowing which way I am heading but the sky was overcast and I had no clue where the sun was. I checked the map and found that I had been walking for a good forty five minutes in completely the wrong direction.

The day was already due to be the longest so far at seventeen miles and with an inadvertent diversion was now probably going to be as long as any on the whole walk.

Never mind, I was in good spirits as I headed back into miserable Rosny. I remembered how exhausted I felt circling Rutland Water without a decent break a few months previously. Even if it was going to be a long day, it was important to stop for rest and for food. I saw a decent *boulangerie* when I passed through the town for the first time and considered yet another baguette. Then I spotted a Greek kebab house. Perfect.

The menu on the wall showed faded pictures of every variety of kebab imaginable. I settled for what I knew. Somewhat paler, and even fattier, than those in Oadby's chip shops, the glistening doner kebab oozed irresistibly on its spit.

The comedy-moment came when the kebab man asked if I wanted all the salad options. Next to me stood another customer and his son and they saw me struggle to explain. I understood enough to know that the customer said "He's not French!" to the kebab man.

I smiled weakly and pointed to the onions, which I didn't particularly want.

"Sans... " my mind went blank. I tried a bit of Franglais, "Sans onions?" then added weakly, "En français?"

"Oignons!" said the kebab man and everyone laughed. I realised that I was probably more mentally and physically fatigued that I had thought.

Within minutes I was served an enormous kebab and chips. I polished off the lot. It was a good move. I was finding it much better to eat a larger meal in the day and to snack at night. Not only did it give me energy when I needed it but I had discovered it could be tricky to find a restaurant near the *Formule 1* hotels.

Leaving Rosny for a second time I walked an hour to the even more worn-out Rolleboise. These grey towns along the Seine are on the old trunk road and I could imagine how they once thrived with busy long-distance drivers stopping for rest and refreshment. Now the A13 motorway takes nearly all the through-traffic so their restaurants, hotels and shops have almost all closed.

Bonnières-sur-Seine was a little prettier and Bennecourt,

across the river and off the old main road, even better.

I have already mentioned how the Seine meanders across Normandy from Paris in a crazy way. The outside of each bend cuts deep into the landscape, leaving a steep escarpment, whereas the inside is usually a more gentle slope. It had made for a varied and much more attractive walk than I had predicted. As a family, we have holidayed in France many times, usually much farther south, and I had assumed that the rural scenery of Normandy would be a bit dull. Being close to the river helped of course, there was usually a barge or two to look at. But there really was lots to look at in the ordinary lives being lived out around me in every town, street and field.

I stopped when a tractor pulled off the road in front of me and into a field of barley and rape. The driver aligned it carefully and unfurled its spindly spraying booms like an enormous insect, discharging its pesticide as it set off. I was only yards away and had to walk through the mist, so clutched a handkerchief to my face to avoid exacerbating my sore throat. I was learning to look at the ordinary details with proper curiosity.

After Bonnieres, I walked uphill on a quiet road towards Limetz. This was more like it. The hills and valleys stretched out before me, cows grazed in the fields and for the first time on my walk the sound of the wind in the fresh leaves of the trees was the loudest thing I heard. Limetz is a pretty villlage with narrow streets and an ancient church. I felt I had finally entered rural France and left the Parisian outskirts.

From Limetz I took the narrow road to Giverny, famous as the village chosen by impressionist painter Claude Monet for his home. Apparently Monet was riding a slow train and saw the beautiful village from the window and resolved to settle there. He built a house, planted extensive gardens and painted many of his most famous works there, including the paintings of water lilies in the lake fed by the River Epte.

I arrived from the south, at what I presumed was Monet's back garden. Through tiny gaps in the tall fence I glimpsed wonderful lawns, the flowing stream and many willows. It looked idyllic, a perfect painter's paradise.

As I turned the corner, I took a photograph of the magnificent house. Only later did I realise that this wasn't Monet's house at all. His was farther along, on the opposite side of the road and wasn't half as attractive. I fancied that the owner of the first house was a better gardener than Monet but that he couldn't paint for toffee.

What I couldn't understand was Monet's choice of colour scheme. His house is a garish shade of pink, the same as the huge yet bizarre house on Gartree Road in Oadby, which is spoken of derisively by everyone I know. I wondered about Monet, and why a genius with the palette would get it so wrong with a seven inch brush and a can of masonry paint.

Monet's home and gardens are now open to the public, though I didn't have time to visit. It was late in the day and I still had a long way to go. There were surprisingly few visitors; just one coach and a handful of cars. It seemed the perfect time of year to visit. The leaves were of so many subtle shades and everything was lush and growing. The gentle drizzle that fell lent everything a special tranquillity and brought fresh scents from the flowers.

Walking the path along the old railway track, I thought of Monet on his train during his first visit, his head pressed against the window and his mind spinning with possibilities. It is a charming place.

The path brought me all the way into Vernon, where they make the engines that power the mighty *Ariane* rocket at the SNECMA factory which is hidden among the trees on the escarpment. Apparently the town was first mentioned by Pepin the Short, King of the Franks, in 750. I wondered if Pepin had to endure a lot of sniggering every time his name was announced in the court.

Even though it's a large town, Vernon still has a sense of history and a certain confidence that is long gone from the by-passed towns which I saw earlier in the day.

As I shopped for supplies at *Lidl*, the rain turned from a steady drizzly to a torrential downpour. I was tired and foolishly didn't put on waterproofs, thinking that I might as well plod on to the journey's end. In fact, the walk to the hotel took another fifty minutes and I was drenched when I got to reception. The man at the desk looked up and down the bedraggled hiker with a *Lidl* bag who stood dripping in front of him.

It seemed like a good moment to begin my story, of who I was and where I was going. He was very kind and when I asked for the most peaceful room, obliged happily.

I changed into fresh gear and showered as usual, and lay on the bed to work out how far I had come. During eight and a half hours of walking, I had covered twenty miles. That was sixty-five altogether - about an eighth of the total. With the treat of a day off before me, I felt I had accomplished a lot. The nervous beginnings in Paris already felt a long way behind me, new routines had emerged and the walk was teaching me its own rhythm.

The only downside was that the large supermarket next door to the hotel had already closed by the time I had got changed. Instead of a warming meal, I sat down to eat some bread and ham, using the spectacularly sharp knife from the camping set that I had bought in Leicester. This little cutlery set included a folding knife, spoon and fork, all of which clipped together neatly and were stowed in a pouch. I had wondered about buying a plastic set to save on weight but the man in the shop insisted that the stainless steel version, which was on special offer, would be ideal.

The fork and spoon, while working adequately, were a little on the feeble side. But the knife looked like a fearsome weapon. Its pointed blade was razor sharp but what lent it a menacing air, apart from the drilled holes in the handle, was the locking mechanism. I was pretty sure that this was the sort of knife that I had seen on television news bulletins where serious-faced police officers poured out the contents of a large plastic bin during a knife amnesty. I spread my baguette with cream cheese like a gangster might.

It was a wonderful feeling. To know that I didn't have to walk another mile on a day off and that the supermarket next door to the hotel was big enough to look after my every need.

Today's walking verse was Leviticus 26.13, *I am the Lord your God who brought you out of the land of Egypt, to be their slaves no more; I have broken the bars of your yoke and made you walk erect.*

During the day I had been pondering ideas of captivity and liberty. I thought of the escaped British prisoners of war and airmen shot down in the fields of northern France. They had to travel by night and navigate without the GPS-enabled mobile phone and maps that I carried. All the time their one goal was to get home.

Those wartime escapees had, in one sense already found their freedom. But they still hid and worked their way furtively and fearfully through Normandy to the coast. In the fullest sense, they wouldn't be truly liberated until they were home in Britain.

The Israelites addressed by God in Leviticus had already been delivered from slavery in Egypt under Pharaoh's cruel regime. But the question remained about how free they really were. The verse reminds them that they were liberated to be truly free, walking out in the open with a head-held-high dignity.

The story of God's people is of a constant falling short of realising that real freedom, of falling back into ways of living that hold people captive. I wondered about the people I had met during the day, especially those who walked with heads down, wearing expressions that betrayed inner fears or sorrows. What, I wondered, would truly liberating freedom look like for these?

–

Day Six was a rest day spent entirely within a couple of hundred yards of the hotel. I visited the café for a breakfast of croissant and proper coffee. And at lunch time I returned for a delicious plate of skate wings in a caper sauce. It was all very reasonably priced and very busy too. Business people, as well as shoppers, filled the restaurant. I relaxed and ordered a second glass of treacly *Leffe* beer, whose dark taste reminded me of a childhood cough medicine.

I should really have visited historic Vernon but the town centre was almost an hour's walk from the hotel and, frankly, I wanted a break. Besides, the clouds had built themselves to the point of tipping heavy showers into the area and I didn't fancy another soaking. Mellowed by the *Leffe*, I lay down in my room and slept through the afternoon. This was a mistake, as I struggled to get to sleep at night.

I had plenty of time to ponder Deuteronomy 10.12 as I lay awake: *So now, O Israel, what does the Lord your God require of you? Only to fear the Lord your God, to walk in all his ways, to love him, to serve the Lord your God with all your heart and with all your soul...*

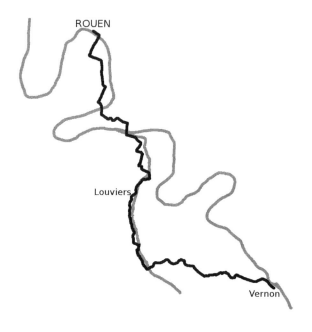

Vernon to Rouen - 47 miles turning north and following the River Eure before rejoining the Seine

Chapter Two - Vernon to Rouen

The next four-day leg of my walk would take me westwards from Vernon and the Seine into the Eure *département*, then in a northerly route to Rouen. This had been one of the trickiest sections of the route to plan, the hotels being difficult to arrange into an evenly spaced itinerary. I had finally settled on three long walks and a fourth shorter one to complete the set. In terms of distance it looked like a good plan but I had little expectation that the scenery would be interesting. As it turned out, this leg scored well on both accounts.

I didn't sleep until one thirty am, owing to the afternoon nap that followed lunch. I felt groggy when I headed back into the supermarket for breakfast. Still, I was packed up and on the road by nine-forty, which was pretty good.

The day's walk was between two rivers, the Seine and the Eure. In between lay a stretch of higher ground, with no major road routes. This meant I could walk for the first time on country footpaths as well as tiny lanes. In fact, there would be no towns of any significant size during the day, just small villages and settlements.

I worked my way through ordinary residential roads and at the end of a cul-de-sac found the footpath that would take me into the hills. It was already hot and humid. The weight of a full water bladder in my backpack, as well as some supplies for lunch, made it a harder climb than I had expected.

So it was serendipitous that today's walking verse was 1 Samuel 17.39: *David strapped Saul's sword over the armour and he tried in vain to walk, for he was not used to them. Then David said to Saul, "I cannot walk with these...", so he removed them.*

The passage is written humorously - we are meant to see the situation as absurd. Not only is the impending fight between young David and the mighty Goliath a total mismatch but the boy can't even dress himself for battle. I can imagine David's feeble reply when the royal armourer asked how it feels to wear the best armour in the kingdom: "I can't walk!"

By comparison, my pack had been working very well and the equipment had proven itself excellently. I even found a use for the bulldog clips that I brought (much to the amusement of friends) by making a clothes line for my hotel room.

Deciding what I needed to carry wasn't easy. One of my character flaws is my desire to be prepared for all eventualities, though interestingly I only lasted two weeks in the Boy Scouts. (They didn't tell me when I signed up that I would be expected to go to church - just one visit to a dismal service was enough to convince me at the age of seven that scouting and church-going were not for me). In preparing for the walk I was tempted to equip myself with every conceivable gadget and trinket. One of the things I had already learned from the sabbatical was to rely more on God's providence. It was really okay not to be prepared for every eventuality.

I imagine the horror on the faces of David's compatriots as he struggled out of the armour, lay down the massive sword and instead readied himself for the fight with the giant Goliath with his simple sling and five smooth stones from the stream. In the end of course, his courage and faith saw him through to victory, there wasn't really any need for much else.

Rather than carry bottles of water I had followed the advice of Paula, another walking vicar friend. She suggested a *Platypus hydration system*, which consists of a tough plastic bladder and a length of blue pipe onto which a teat with a bite-valve was fixed. My rucksack had an internal pocket specially designed for a water bladder, and a little opening marked "H_2O" for the tube to exit the pack. I could run the pipe onto my right shoulder strap where a elasticated fabric band held the teat. To begin with it had felt odd to drink by biting the teat and slurping but by Day Seven I had grown accustomed to it.

The practical benefit of having a mouthful of water every few minutes was immense. Carrying a bottle in my bag would have inevitably meant that I would drink less often than I should, and that the less frequent drinks would each be comparatively large. Apparently this is not good. It chills the stomach and plays havoc with digestion. The trusty *Platypus* hardly let me down during the whole walk. (There was a moment, hundreds of miles after I left Vernon, when I bit a little enthusiastically and pulled the teat from the end of the tube. Fortunately, I was able to refit it and carry on).

I had become a little concerned that the tap water that I was filling my *Platypus* with was contributing to the sore throat, which by now was becoming a real problem. I didn't want to catch a cold, so I was hoping that it was simply a result of hay fever, or dust on the roads. But by now I was wondering if the water in the cheap hotels was properly clean or whether I had acquired an infection. I washed the Platypus each day but on this day, for extra protection, I decided to use an antibacterial wipe from my first aid kit on the mouthpiece. I left Vernon with a nasty taste in my mouth.

The shade offered by the trees in the little wood of Bois-de-Saint-Just was very welcome on the steep slope. For the first time I was walking on soil and for the first time I probably looked like my outfit matched the terrain. I had been liberal with the sunscreen and was glad for a hat that kept the bright sun from my eyes.

Once onto the level ground of the plateau, I joined a quiet road which ran along the perimeter of the Orwellian-sounding *National Centre for Prevention and Protection*, an extensive complex enclosed behind eight-feet fencing, topped with barbed wire and two further coils of razor wire beneath. I looked it up on the internet when I reached my destination and found that it does research into fire safety and other risks. Curious then, that there's so much security. I wondered what else they did there.

The "No Admittance" signs warned of surveillance patrols and sure enough I was passed by a leather-jacketed driver who turned around a few hundred metres along the road and came past again, taking a good look at me. I thought it prudent to take no photographs.

Villez-sous-Bailleul, like the other hamlets I passed through, had no shop or cafe. I lunched, in a bus shelter in Champenard, on a delicious goat's cheese and bacon sandwich that I had picked up from the supermarket next to the hotel.

The road across the Plain des Noes took me through huge fields of yellow rape and green wheat beneath a wide sky. Farther on, above La Lié, there was a glorious cloudscape. Towering cumulus nimbus clouds were growing ever taller against a background of mare's tails and little cumulus humilis scuttled along in front.

Several times I paused, not only to rest but to take in the sheer beauty of the places through which I was walking. I've never seen France this way. This was the *bocage,* a landscape of pastures and woodlands, of birds and flowers and steep thatched roofs. The sheer lushness of it all was amazing, everything alive and growing.

One consequence of taking the paths away from the Seine is that I climbed more hills than I had so far. The whole walk for the day was 13.5 miles but it felt longer due to the up-and-down terrain. Although I had got better at judging the amount of water to carry, hauling my pack took some effort.

I descended the slopes on the western side of the plateau along a bumpy unpaved track, just as rain began to fall. It took me a while to find the *Auberge des Deux Sapins* in pretty Cailly-sur-Eure but it was a lovely change from the *Formule 1* experience.

My room had its own bathroom and shower. Perhaps it was the thrill of this luxury, or my tiredness at the end of a long hot day, that led me into a calamity that could have ended the walk. I had run the shower, undressed and stepped in. As I did so, my left foot slipped and I stumbled, my right shin bearing my whole weight onto the ceramic edge of the shower basin.

"Ouch! That's going to bruise!" I said to myself.

Even as I washed, I could feel the swelling starting to grow. By the time I had dried myself, the leg was very tender. I swallowed a couple of Ibuprofen tablets and tried to be brave. I ate every morsel of a three-course dinner, amazed by my capacity to eat - I didn't think I was particularly hungry - and washed it down with a half-carafe of the house red. This dulled the pain of my leg and having had less than six hours sleep the previous night I fell asleep in the closing moments of the Champions League match between Manchester United and Arsenal.

–

I began Day Eight by breakfasting with Ron and Mike, two

retired Brits whose hotel room was just down the corridor from me. They were returning to London having spent two months in Montpellier on their barge, the *Osseo*.

"Do you know Longfellow?", asked Ron.

I half-remembered something about Hiawatha but shook my head.

"Osseo was the magician," explained Mike. "We named our barge after him."

Ron and Mike were rather sunburned and rather camp, good company and delightfully odd in a refined kind of way.

"You'd like a friend of ours," said Ron, "he's a very spiritual man."

I wondered if I would.

We spent an hour comparing France and the UK, with France generally scoring better on a range of topics. We talked about the health services in particular. France has a very high ratio of doctors to the population and it sometimes seems that the French worry more about their health than anything else. I was interested, just in case my leg, which was displaying all the colours of summer fruits when I woke up, might need some expert attention.

"I had a rash on my arm last year," said Ron.

"He'd been bitten", explained Mike.

"I went to the French doctor just to make sure it was okay. He suggested I see a top skin specialist immediately and rang her while I was in his consulting room. He asked her to wait for a moment, and asked me if I could get to her in the next half-hour. Imagine that happening in the UK!"

Ron went on to say that he underwent every kind of test imaginable and that when he left he was given a twenty-five page dossier on his health that amazed his British doctor.

When Mike went into hospital for a minor condition they kept him there for three weeks. "We had to threaten them with arranging an air ambulance back to the UK, just to get him out!", said Ron.

Mike and Ron have travelled the world all their lives. Mike as a ship's engineer and Ron in the airline industry. After retirement twenty years ago they bought their Dutch barge and have sailed the canals all across Western Europe together ever since.

"You should try walking the canals." said Ron. "They all have towpaths and we see lots of walkers."

I promised I would check the maps again but I was pretty sure that my route didn't include any canals until I reached Worcester. We wished each other well and said our goodbyes.

It was a straightforward day's walk - twelve miles, bringing my total so far to ninety. Thankfully, although my leg was very tender to the touch, whatever damage I had done to my shin didn't hurt any more or less whether I walked or remained still. Rather than taking the *Route National* as initially planned, I switched to the west bank of the Eure, which is one of a small number of rivers in France that flow from south to north.

In 1 Kings 3.14 King Solomon hears, in a dream, God's response to his prayer for wisdom: *If you will walk in my ways, keeping my statutes and commandments, as your father David walked, then I will lengthen your life.*

"Staying on track," "sticking to the path," "keeping to the straight and narrow." We use these expressions all the time and they are rooted in various parts of the Bible. The message is a consistent one; there is a right way to walk and a wrong way to walk. I prayed that I would be led home in God's ways.

Heudreville-sur-Eure was a rather posh little village, and in its tiny store I bought a quiche and a baguette, which I strapped to the back of my rucksack. It made me look, I fancied, more like a French hiker. As I left, I sensed I was going to be the topic of conversation for the staff and customers for a while. They had clearly regarded me as a little odd. I walked on, past more fields and through the strung-out town of Acquigny. Here, every second house had a snarling dog.

Dogs had er... dogged me for most of my walk so far. It appeared to me that the French love them even more than the British. It's a love which I confess I don't share.

Parisians have silly little dogs, which they carry in specially made holders. The dog's head peeps out while the owner takes it for a walk, though its feet never touch the ground. Out in the country, the dogs are larger, fiercer and louder. They guard their owner's property behind high walls and fences which allow the dog just enough sight of the passer-by to arouse their fury.

Come to think about it, I had seen only a few passers-by in all my journey, so I imagine my appearance had delivered a treat to every hound on my walk.

The presence of a vicious guard dog is often, but not always, marked with a plaque on the gate "Attention. Chien Méchant!" I passed a property with no fence or gate; instead the slavering hound was tied to a tree by a long rope. Above it was nailed a skull-and-crossbones sign. I got the message.

The dogs are usually dozing as I approach and I often startled them by my footsteps when I was virtually at their door. They look ashamed to have been caught off-guard and channel their rage into even greater vocal ferocity. Sometimes, though, it's the dogs that surprise me and I am jolted from distracted thoughts by the sound of bounding paws and furious barking, which brings every other dog in the neighbourhood into the chorus.

I was slowly getting used to the canine dangers but while approaching Louviers, something else happened that frightened me out of my skin. I was walking along the pavement when I was very nearly hit by a car. (Actually, that is exaggerating the danger a little. I was very nearly hit by *a piece* of a car.)

I was reading my map at the time when I heard a bang, and a loud metallic scraping sound. A *Renault Clio* was passing me quickly and its wheel trim detached itself and was skidding along in my direction. I skipped to the side and let it roll past. The driver didn't bother to stop.

Louviers is a delightful town, with a pretty but rather unkempt church in the centre. The structure is supported by the thinnest of flying buttresses and the stonework is very delicate. There are many fine half-timbered buildings in Louviers and the river in the town centre made for an attractive setting, spoilt by an angry young drunk who looked a bit like an unleashed Chien Méchant himself.

I had by now become a bit of a connoisseur of a very specific piece of architecture - the bus shelter. In Northern France they are mostly equipped with a seat, which makes for a very welcome resting spot for the weary walker. Some are kept in a very tidy state, others are so dusty that they look long neglected. And many bear inscriptions of occupants. Some of these scrawlings are predictable enough - names, insults, political slogans. But others are more baffling. I recorded a pithy, clever-looking piece of writing in my notebook, thinking that I had look it up on the internet and post it to my blog. I couldn't find it at the time, so decided I had not post it on the blog for the world to see, just in case it was offensive. I now know that it was as shockingly rude as anything I could imagine.

Leaving Louviers on the disappointingly busy D343, I passed a prehistoric *menhir* or standing stone. It was good to be able to cross the road, to take my time to look and touch it, wondering about the ancient peoples who erected it here and for what purpose. A little lost in these musings, I barely noticed that a van pulled up a few metres away along the road. The driver got out and urinated against the hedge around the *menhir*, without any concern for my presence.

I decided to take a detour onto a quieter country road that led past a wonderful chateau, which was also a stud farm for beautiful chestnut brown horses. The road dropped down into the outskirts of Le Vaudreuil, where another *Formule 1* was waiting for me.

My right leg was badly swollen by now, the day's twelve miles having done nothing to help it recover from the injury in the previous night's fall. The skin wasn't broken, thankfully. But as well as the swelling, the flesh had turned dark blue, with a magenta fringe to the bruise. I was getting concerned and swallowed more Ibuprofen. I lay sideways across the bed so that I could rest my foot high up on the wall, hoping that this would drain some of the swollen tissue. It made no difference.

After showering and changing I crossed the nearby dual carriageway for dinner at a nearby restaurant. The waitress told me the dish of the day and, when I responded with a blank look, explained that it was a fish. Having left my phrase book in the hotel, I trusted that it would be something edible. In the first few days of the walk I craved sweet sugary food, presumably because of a calorie deficit and my body's desire for cheap energy. But this had given way in the last few days to a craving for fish. Perhaps I needed the protein.

When the dish came I very much enjoyed it; the mystery fish was white and toothsome, firm in texture and delicately flavoured. When the waitress came to collect my plate, I asked her to repeat the name, so that I could look it up when I got back to the hotel. I might even be able to get this delicious fish in England, I thought.

She told me it was called *cabillaud*. I looked it up eagerly when I returned to my bedroom. It turned out to be cod!

—

The swelling on my right leg was no better when I woke on Day Ten. During the night I had started to worry that if it worsened I might have to rest up for a while. This was one of my most feared scenarios for the walk, only slightly less terrifying than getting run down by a lorry or mugged. (I suppose that it now also ranked slightly lower than an encounter in the woods with an angry sex worker.)

My itinerary was working perfectly. I had made good choices when it came to the accommodation and overall route. The daily distances were demanding rather than devastating and having a reservation at a hotel meant that I could enjoy the day as much as possible, without being nervous that I would miss out on a bed for the night. The disadvantage to all the planning was that if I needed a break to recover from illness or injury, I would have to take a train or taxi to resume the walk - there was no other way to catch up.

I realised that if I needed to rest in order to let my leg heal, it would probably involve at least two and more likely three days. A doctor or pharmacist could tell me what I needed to do but after the conversation with Mike and Ron I feared that the French health service might keep me in a hospital ward for a month.

"It's fine!" I told Jennifer on the phone. "Just a bit bruised and swollen."

I assured her that if it got worse I had get some medical help. Concerned messages were appearing in the comments on my blog - it was really touching to know that people cared for my welfare. After all, it was only a badly swollen leg.

The walk for Day Nine was 13.5 miles, taking my aggregate to 103.5 miles, or twenty percent of the total. Interestingly, there was no accompanying sense of achievement, or even of progress. The numbers felt pretty abstract and my horizons had shrunk so that I lost perspective of the overall journey. This wasn't a problem, in fact it was refreshing to be occupied wholly with what I was doing. But I was surprised at the extent to which my outlook had shifted to a 'one day at a time' mentality.

Enough days had passed for me to realise that I was carrying unnecessary ballast. I had accumulated out-of-date paperwork which could be ditched and, with a heavy heart, I decided that Charles Pomerol's excellent guidebook to the *Footpaths of Normandy and The Seine* had to go. It is a fabulous book but I hadn't used the long distance footpaths he described for long enough to make it worthwhile to carry. As I was feeling tired I thought it best to save two hundred grams and ditch it.

I left Val-de-Reuil, a nineteen-seventies new town and

walked past fields of rape and barley. The footpath that I had chosen to take me up into the trees was blocked by construction work and there was no diversion signalled. However, I found my way round to another track which took me up a steep slope into the forest.

The sky was cloudless and as I hadn't left the hotel until eleven o'clock the burning sun was already high in the sky. The yellow fields shimmered in the distance. I applied a second layer of sun cream and took to the shade of the trees.

The wood was full of enchantments. The birds sang louder than any I have ever heard and big black beetles scuttled along the forest floor. Thankfully the clouds of black flies that had followed me through the fields didn't join me in the trees.

I stopped to sit on a fallen trunk and let myself be overwhelmed by all that was happening around me. For the first time on my journey, I saw other recreational walkers. It was a national holiday, *Fête du Travail*, the first of May and a few families were out in the sunshine. Later in the day I would see girls selling posies by the roadside. Many times I saw people visiting friends and families, carrying flowers as gifts.

The walk through the trees was idyllic. It came to a grittier end when I found the footpath to the road at the edge of the forest blocked by more construction work. A new road was being built and before long the path I was on would be carried through a tunnel. It looked easy enough to get through the half-finished tunnel. A high fence with a warning notice about keeping out stood before me. I checked the map and a detour to another track would add another mile or so to my journey. I had gained confidence during the previous week and reckoned I was up for a spot of intrusion.

Being a bank holiday, the excavating machinery was silent and the site looked deserted, so I decided to clamber down a slimy

71

embankment, squeeze through a gap in the fence and cross the sticky mud to the tunnel. I congratulated myself on my daring and was halfway through the dark tube when it occurred to me that the site might be protected with those vicious guard dogs so beloved of the French. My steps quickened. Fortunately there were none and I emerged on the other side.

I had asked at the hotel how many shops would be open during the holiday and was told that very few would do so. I had eaten well the night before and forced a larger quantity of bread and jam down than usual in the morning, just in case the day would be lunch-less. But as I entered the centre of Pont-de-l'Arche I found the central square busy with young men at bars. While the restaurants were shut, two kebab shops were open. I decided to join the youngsters in the nearest.

I ordered a *kebab panini*, a first for me, and a small bottle of *1664* lager. It was all delicious. I chatted in faltering French with the Moroccan owner, who told me his son lives in Manchester. I showed him my route and he was impressed. "Courage!" he said.

I crossed the Seine for the seventh-and-a-half time (calculating that the start point at Notre-Dame cathedral is on the Ile-de-la-Cité, so only scores half a crossing) and found myself in Igoville. A nice name for a bit of a dull town. Local youths were enjoying themselves racing their *Renault Clios* and *Peugot 205s* around the empty supermarket car park. They screeched their tyres, played loud music and shouted to each other through open windows. Every so often, one of these wannabe-gangsters would pass me at speed on the road, sounding their horn and jeering.

The map showed a promising route away from the main road, so I slogged uphill for a mile and a half. It allowed me to catch an occasional and spectacular view across the wide valley to the forest through which I had walked in the morning. Despite the beauty of the valley, the plateau at the top was ugly. Dirty industrial buildings, scrap yards and dishevelled horses stood in fields either side of the pot-holed track.

I checked the map and it confirmed that I was on a walking route, along a *communaux* or common land. It would take me through a travellers' camp, where caravans, vans and Mercedes cars were parked. All the vehicles were white, and all were spotlessly clean. I wasn't troubled by anyone but the man at the gate who was tending a ferocious fire looked wary. I gave him a big, broad smile and a hearty "Bonjour!"

I got a grudging reply as I stepped carefully over his chickens.

The wide grin was a new technique of mine for disarming the French. It had become apparent that they are unsure of me and what I was doing. My routes took me down quiet residential roads, along farm tracks and busy highways, so I didn't look like the normal tourist. Defying categorisation, I was disturbing the peace.

I remember hearing that when travelling in far-flung parts of the world a smile gets you a long way. There is something primitive and essential about non-verbal communication and I had come to realise that when nervous I probably can't help communicating my insecurity to those around me.

So with a big smile I had started to bid people, "Bonjour!"

To begin with, I was half-hearted about it. But in the evenings I had enjoyed watching a French TV programme in which a solo traveller, wired with cameras and microphone, ventures into remote communities around the world and tries to befriend the natives. I think the title of the programme is something like, *Can I sleep at your house?* It's brilliant television and it hardly mattered that I only understood every fifth word. The presenter's best asset was his winning smile and it was amazing how often people responded to him with generosity and hospitality. This, I thought, was worth a go.

After my beaming greeting, the strangers I met instinctively smiled back, albeit with an uncertain look. My imbecilic grin seemed to be working.

On this bank holiday, even Tourville's huge *Ikea* store was closed. In France recreation involves dining with one's family, or at least hanging with one's friends in chavvy cars. In Britain it requires shopping.

In Oissel I saw nineteenth-century terraced houses, some of them four-stories of rooms around a Dickensian courtyard. The bricks were dirty and the windows and doors grimy but there were families living in them. It was a little glimpse into the kind of slum housing that existed in many cities before the high-rise blocks were built.

I crossed the Seine again (eight and a half times now) and noted how broad it had become. It was easily three times as wide as in Paris and, with its waters swollen by the Eure, was now a mighty river.

The directions for my hotel on the edge of Saint Étienne du Vouvray required an approach via the *Rond Point aux Vaches*. Had I got that right, the roundabout of cows? In Leicester we have a "Pork Pie Roundabout," so named because of the circular pastry-coloured brick library that lies on its edge. I trudged through the streets and, sure enough, came upon a roundabout populated with life-size plastic cows.

This was my first night in a *Hotel Premiére Classe*, my preferred French budget hotel chain. Unlike the more common *Formule 1*, *Premiére Classe* rooms have their own showers and toilets and, best of all, free wifi connections.

This was a real blessing as I had been spending far more than I had planned on dial-up internet access through my mobile phone. For some reason, the costs had been strangely unpredictable; some days I had spent less than a pound, on others fifteen.

I dined at the neighbouring hotel on another white fish, though I wasn't sure of the exact variety. It made a welcome change from chips. This was accompanied by a very quaffable carafe of *Vin de Pays Rouge*.

At the till I got talking with a family from Rotherham, who were setting off to begin a six-week holiday in the south of France. I swapped email addresses with Melanie, who told me she would be reading my blog from now on.

It was especially good to talk with Jennifer, who was beginning a week-long holiday with two of her friends in Malaga. She must have flown above me during the day. Our family had never been so scattered.

My walking verse for Day Nine was 1 Kings 8.23: *Solomon said, "O Lord, god of Israel, there is no god like you in heaven above or on earth beneath, keeping covenant and steadfast love for your servants who walk before you with all their heart."*

–

I had made it to Day Ten. Mark Moxon was absolutely right: I was worn out. But I trusted in his promise that somewhere between the second and third weeks, my rising fitness levels would overtake my fatigue.

The first thing I did after waking was to fling the covers back and to check my right leg for any signs of further deterioration. It didn't seem any worse, except for the colour, and I thought that the swelling might be reducing. I could now feel the bone of my ankle joint, even though it wasn't visible beneath the blobby flesh. The injury was higher up my leg but most of the colourful fluid had seeped through the tissues into my foot. The whole area was mostly a pale greyish yellow but there were spectacular reds, blues and purples lower down.

In planning the route I knew I wanted to spend Sunday in Rouen, Normandy's capital city, but the scattering of cheap hotels created an unavoidable unequal division of distances. The walk for Day Ten, at slightly less than seven miles, was half the length of the previous day.

The shorter distance was very welcome for my aching body but I predicted it wasn't going to be spectacular, as it would simply lead me through the suburbs of Rouen, northwards to one of its five bridges across the Seine to my hotel. It would be my first walk through city suburbs since Paris and I remembered how tough they could be and how unsettled I had felt in them.

So with comparatively low expectations I set off after a late start. It was pavement all the way but it felt surprisingly good, like I was joining in with a normal French Saturday.

I waited in the long queue in a pharmacy to buy some more Ibuprofen and enjoyed the mixture of neighbourhood shops in Sotteville. Farther on, a very friendly greengrocer helped me choose the ripest of peaches. They wouldn't have been given shelf-space in a British supermarket for they were small and pock-marked. They tasted delicious!

Sitting under a tree and enjoying the wonderful fruit, I reckoned that the day was already turning out much better than expected. Then a bird pooped on me! I laughed. Out loud. And I noticed how little it mattered to me and how delightfully trivial it was. In the ten days I had been walking I was much more relaxed and ready to take whatever came my way.

I couldn't really make much of a personal connection with my walking verse from Esther 2.11: *Every day Mordecai would walk around the court of the harem, to learn how Esther was and how she fared.*

I have visions of Mordecai pacing up and down, anxious to find out if his cousin Esther was alright. The story of Esther is a wonderful account of an heroic girl and of evil being overcome through her integrity and resilience. God is never in the foreground, barely mentioned in fact, but it's apparent that in the workings of circumstance his purposes are fulfilled. It's sometimes hard to know God's presence. But that's okay. God doesn't need me to experience anything special when I pray. Like Mordecai and Esther, for the most part walking with God is about hanging in there, putting in the miles and trusting that all will be well.

St Sever, on the Rive Gauche which is the south side of the Seine opposite Rouen, was busy with shoppers. It's a cosmopolitan place and, perhaps because it lies in the shadow of its more attractive neighbour, it felt like a no-nonsense kind of town. I bought a punnet of strawberries and walked up to the bridge where I thought I might find a quiet spot by the river.

Then came my next surprise. The bridge was packed with people and I walked to the parapet to see what the fuss was about. Beneath me lay something akin to a Formula 1 pit lane. Beyond some hospitality tents a row of temporary structures lined the bank of the river and just visible in each was the nose of a powerboat. Five cranes stood ready to hoist the craft into the water. A fabulous ten-piece band entertained the crowd.

I had arrived at the start of the annual Rouen twenty-four hour powerboat race. After changing at my hotel, I set off to find out more.

By this time the race had just begun. Thousands of people were pouring into the centre of Rouen, lining the banks and bridges four or five deep. I tried to work out what was happening. The boats race around the Ile Lacroix in the centre of the river, and there appeared to be two classes of craft, one taking a line closer to the island and the other passing outer marker buoys nearer to the riverbank where I stood.

The boats were tiny and the drivers' heads bounced as they steered their craft across the waves and wakes. The outboard engines screamed away from the turns, lifting the front of the boats as they flew eastwards again under the bridges.

After an hour watching the powerboat race, I left the noise of the river and headed for the cathedral. I walked first to the western façade, having seen Monet's studies of it in the Musée d'Orsay in Paris. The stonework was beautifully crafted and contrasted with the plain interior. But the cathedral's most striking feature is its spire. The stone tower is topped with an amazingly delicate Gothic spike, so sharp and elegant. In fact, this is an iron-and-steel spire made in the twentieth century and replaced at least three previous wooden spires which were covered with gilded lead and all of which suffered destruction by fire.

The cathedral has certainly seen tough times. In 1944 it was badly bombed as part of the allied air raids on Rouen in preparation for D-Day. A display panel in the south aisle told how in the 1990s a tornado tore away a pinnacle of the tower, which fell over a hundred feet and embedded itself in the roof of the nave, causing a partial collapse.

Tired but not completely exhausted, bruised but not beaten, I had walked from Paris to Rouen. Perhaps Englishman James Moore felt the same when he arrived here from Paris in 1869, having won the very first cycle road race between any two cities in the world.

–

It was a real treat waking in the knowledge that I didn't have any more walking during the day. But I couldn't give myself a late start, I had to wake at the usual time to get ready for a live interview with John Florance of BBC Radio Leicester. He was very interested in my misadventures in the forest of course, but also gave me a chance to talk about why I was undertaking a pilgrimage-in-reverse.

I enjoyed the radical architecture of the church of Joan of Arc. It is only thirty years old and ranks as the most unusual church building that I have seen. Joan was burned to death on the site by the English in 1431, aged nineteen. She was canonized as a saint in the Roman Catholic Church, as late as 1920. Joan has become an icon of French heroism, treasured as an embodiment of the fierce individual resistance to oppressive power. In different ages, the mythology of Joan has been revived to reflect the priorities of the time. She has become, in turns, a revolutionary, a resistance fighter, a nationalist.

Photographs of the controversial church didn't help me understand how the building fits in its setting. The scheme combines the church itself, a covered market and a memorial to Joan, who was burned on a stake at the very spot. It's very striking, provocative and I admire the courage behind its construction. No such church could ever be built in the United Kingdom.

Beatification, the Catholic Church's process of making saints, is a hit and miss process. No mortal is wholly virtuous and it's a risky business to make a model and example out of someone at the high tide of a posthumous popularity. The idea that particular saints make interventions with God seems a bit peculiar to say the least. There's no convincing basis for it in the Bible, as far as I can tell. On the contrary, the New Testament points to the sheer grace of God's loving interest in each of us, with no one commending us to him but Jesus Christ. Anything else seems irrelevant and superfluous to me.

So I didn't ask Joan to pray for me, nor did I light a candle at her shrines. And no, I didn't carry a medallion of St Christopher, the patron saint of travellers, who was reputed to have carried an almost impossibly heavy child across a river, only to discover that this was the Christ-child. It strikes me that Christopher did well in landing such a plum patronage, especially in our mobile modern age. His medallions dangle in millions of cars and in Spain, often bear the inscription: *Si en San Cristóbal confías, de accidente no morirás* (If you trust St. Christopher, you won't die in an accident). I have to say that I had prefer to ride with a driver who relied less on a saint and more on the *Highway Code*.

This would be a good point to say something about pilgrimage. After all, I was walking at least partly in the tradition of centuries of religious people, who set off on long journeys in the hope of gaining some spiritual benefit.

It's natural to want to see the place where something significant took place. To 'stand on the spot' of a momentous event is to experience a connection with it in some deep way. This is a universal human phenomenon. Places acquire special significance and for all the books, films and pictures that describe and show us special places, there's no substitute for being there.

It is often declared that tourism grew out of pilgrimage but I wonder if it's the other way round - that at it's most basic, pilgrimage is about simply 'standing on the spot where it happened', whatever 'it' might be.

No wonder the earliest followers of Jesus wanted to visit the Holy Land. The Bible is not an abstract philosophy or a list of things to be done and things to be avoided. It's the collected experience of people relating to God, a narrative of adventure. Those early believers came to discover God revealed through things happening to particular people, at particular times and in particular places. This is a big point for anyone who's serious about discovering more about the life of faith: it isn't enough to distil some abstract Christian principles from the stuff of life. Christianity is based on a quite scandalously particular set of events, the coming of God in a unique and particular person, who lived and died among a ragbag of ordinary people in ordinary and particular places, and who was raised to life so that ordinary people like us could share in that life together.

Christianity began, and remains today, a religion of location, of place and moment. No wonder that believers wanted to visit the towns, lakes and mountains of the Holy Land, to experience these sites and sights for themselves.

These weren't easy journeys to make, especially in an era when only traders and soldiers travelled farther than a day or two from home. As Christianity spread, the distances for these visitors grew. Difficulty and danger made pilgrimage even more worthwhile and certainly more appealing. The hazardous journey itself became a metaphor for the struggle to live the Christian life: of courage, trust, self denial, faith, purposefulness and hope.

In time, the cult of saintly heroes created a whole range of competing destinations. Monasteries acquired saintly relics: heads, limbs, toenails, and hair. The pilgrim trade grew into an international tour of holy bits and pieces.

The power of relics was also understood to transfer to the keepers, or to the town in which they were stored. So when St Martin died in southern France in 397, on the road between Tours and Poitiers, the two towns fought over his body. The relics of a saint were thought to lend a protection and blessing, so in times of war, famine and disease the relics were considered vital assets for any community.

Visiting the shrine of a saint was also believed to confer a special blessing, and pilgrims would often set off to a particular place in order to receive healing or in the hope of a special revelation or answer to prayer.

Both journey and destination together then, provided a purpose for a pilgrimage. By undertaking an arduous journey, pilgrims put their faith into action, denied themselves whatever comforts and material advantage they normally enjoyed. By reaching their journey's end, they not only realised the thrill of achievement but some spiritual reward.

Of course, this is a bit of a problem for a faith in which divine grace is supreme. The New Testament emphasises that we can't earn our way to blessings, that superstition is at best a distraction and at worst a domestication of God for our own convenience. Pilgrimage risks bending the heart of the Christian disciple away from sheer divine grace towards an endeavour of acquisition, achievement and power.

What did I think I was doing then, going on a pilgrimage for the first time in my life?

I'll answer this first in relation to *destination* and second, *journey.*

A shrine held no appeal for me as the goal of my walk. I saw no value in being somewhere of special religious significance. For the reasons I've described, I expected to gain no blessing or sublime religious experience at a place pre-chosen for a destination. Besides, my heart sinks at the way that the well-known shrines are *owned* by institutional churches of one denominational flavour or another. I don't think I could experience them without feeling angry at the way that access is granted or withheld, as though the wild grace of God has to be tamed and rationed, dispensed decently according to the timetables of a staffed building. "Queue here for your blessing" does not work for me.

Instead I chose to make home, the place where I live and work, my destination. From the idea of a shrine I wanted to borrow the notions of located blessing, of God's presence, of transformational encounter and to put them in their proper place, among the ordinary stuff of the ordinary life that I live among ordinary people. I like where I live and the people I live with.

Likewise, the journey was going to be a way for me to experience a healthy dis-location. This French part, in particular, made me an alien, dis-empowered me and made me vulnerable. I couldn't carry much, I could hardly speak the language, I was defenceless and reliant on how others treated me. Like most people, I usually spend too much time and energy in seeking my own comfort, security and entertainment, living too independently of others. And while parish ministry brings many challenges it also includes the reward of feeling wanted, liked and valuable. These wonderfully encouraging things carry a danger: it's easy for clergy to be seduced into playing to the crowd, to getting their own importance out of proportion. Being on the road and out-of-role was a great way to be ordinary once again.

I chose the English part of the route in order to meet up with friends and family and to re-visit places I had known before. Years pass too easily without re-connecting with people and I wanted to renew friendships. These encounters would also, I hoped, help me to reflect on where I had been, where I was, and where I am heading in my longer life-journey.

Walking home was also a way of relating to the great narrative of the Christian faith. It tells the story of a humanity made in the image of God, made for community with each other and with him. However, that fellowship was soon disrupted by humankind's choice for self-improvement, for independent living and the rejection of our createdness. Humanity became fundamentally estranged, living a poorer version of life in a kind of exile, unable to restore for itself the relationships for which it was made.

In Jesus Christ the possibility for renewal and homecoming was created. Helpless of ourselves, yet still we can be found by God and brought home to the place where we truly belong.

Completing my pilgrimage was therefore not going to be about fulfilling a quest to 'get somewhere' but to be embraced in a homecoming. I didn't want to mark the finish by 'phoning home to say "I've done it!" but to be held by loving arms.

Back to the Church of St Joan. The building itself is a triumph. My one regret is that as I entered at the end of Sunday mass, so few people had worshipped there. I reckoned the congregation was about half of what we would normally expect at St Paul's, Oadby on a regular Sunday.

Inside, the wall behind the altar is almost all glass, retrieved from the church of St Vincent which used to stand on the site and whose members had the foresight to remove their precious glass before the war.

Unlike being in the cathedral yesterday, I felt immediately drawn to pray. Sadly, though, my visit was cut short by the man who was locking the doors. It is disappointing to be asked to leave as one prays and though I understood the building had to be locked, I inwardly fumed. The building had been designed by Auguste Perret to resemble an upturned ship, an ark even. This was an ancient image for the Church, representing the idea of a community on the move, offereing safety to those who risked drowning. Just now, though, it seemed that the welcome was reserved for members of the crew who had turned up at the right time.

My walking verse was Job 18.8. One of Job's less than helpful friends tries to console him about the way things are: *The wicked are thrust into a net by their own feet, and they walk into a pitfall.*

Except that it's not always like that and Job knows it. Bildad the Shuhite (what a great name) tries to resolve the messy brokenness of Job's situation with a pat answer. He declares that the wicked always get themselves into trouble, walking into disaster. Yet Job himself is suffering - and not because of any personal wickedness. Presumably, Bildad has drawn a neat line through the world's population in a way that puts him on the side of the righteous, not the wicked. Professional religionists tend to make a habit of this. I find Job's friends infuriating. They try to explain too much. Job doesn't need to be convinced, he needs companions who simply hang in there with him, people who won't close the doors to him.

During the afternoon I wandered a bit more, checked on the powerboats, which were nearing the end of their twenty-four hour race, watched the tremendously exciting Heineken Cup match between Cardiff and Leicester on television, and napped.

I spent the evening thinking about the visit I would make to Maromme, the twin town of my Borough of Oadby and Wigston. I lay on the bed and took an hour to copy out in longhand the French translation of a little speech I had prepared for the Mayor.

85

My friend Hugh kindly did the hard work of turning my words into French. Now all I had to do was deliver them without sounding like Ted Heath.

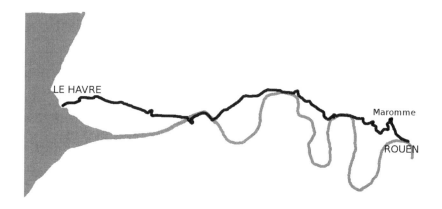

Rouen to Le Havre - 60 miles in the company of the River Seine and out to the English Channel

Chapter Three - Rouen to Le Havre

I felt slightly anxious as I left the hotel and headed west. Perhaps it was apprehension at my meeting with the mayor later in the morning, or perhaps the residual awkwardness from my encounter in a Rouennais street the night before with an inebriated man and woman in the doorway of a down-market cafe. She'd called something to me as I passed. I had tried to explain that I didn't understand and the man cracked a joke, presumably at my expense. She giggled and slapped his chest, smiled at me with a look that combined pity and charity. I laughed without conviction and stepped out of their way. Silly little incidents like this reminded me how far from home I was, how inept I was at handling situations in which not only the language but the code of gesture and glance were obscure to me.

Rouen has a surprisingly large port, big enough to handle modest container vessels, and I passed busy cranes and noisy depots before turning north up through an industrialised valley. This narrow corridor between steep-sided hills had been a convenient location for industries which used the port for importing raw materials and transporting finished goods. The roads ran north-south following the contours and the towns tipped into one another in long ribbons of mixed up development. It had the feel of the South Wales valleys.

Small houses were squeezed between railways and factories, the largest of which made steel pipes. As I walked past, a car pulled up in front of me and the driver got out. Used to people asking for directions, I was ready with my stock response, "Pardon. Je n'habite pas ici." - *sorry, I don't live here.* My thick accent usually convinces people not to persist with the exchange and they leave with what is often described as a Gallic shrug.

This car driver smiled however, and explained in reasonable English that he was a walker too. He told me that he saw me use my GPS phone to check my route. He was planning a trip to the Alps and was interested in getting one for himself. We had a good chat about the technology and its limitations. I explained that the GPS facility on my phone is not so good in city centres and even on very cloudy days it can take a long time to get a signal accurate enough to know my location. We also talked about Leatherhead, of all places, where he worked in a restaurant for a couple of years. He was keen to understand my journey and I showed him my route plan. With a "Bon Chance!" he was off and I returned to the walk north.

Forging international civic relations is something with which I'm not much experienced. It occurred to me that the Mayor of Maromme had probably even less idea about the meeting that was, hopefully, in his diary for that morning. With such limited skills in French at my disposal I wanted our encounter to be constructive to the *entente cordiale*.

I had arranged the appointment with the help of Councillor Jill Gore, the Mayor of Oadby and Wigston. A few weeks before the walk began, I met an ex-councillor of Oadby who told me that some time in the nineteen eighties there was a civic exchange trip.

However, the fashion for twinning, once all the rage, seems to have diminished. Perhaps council tax-payers had begun to ask questions about the precise value of sending local officials to fact-find. Yet without at least periodic re-connection town-twinning slips into a curious combination of publicly proclaimed relationship and everyday forgetfulness. The twinning signs are as public as the name of a girlfriend tattooed on a lover's wrist - impressive marks of commitment when a relationship is hot, rather awkwardly visible when it's gone cold.

After the wooing period of twinning has faded, of course, it's very hard to undo the connection. Even if a pair of twin-towns recognise that the relationship has effectively ended, that it would be nice to reclaim the space on the "Welcome to Anytown" sign for a message about safe driving or progress in last year's *Britain in bloom* award, it's a delicate matter to break the link. Who, exactly,would pick up the phone first. What would they say? *Er, hi it's Anytown here. Look, this twinning thing, it's not really working for either of us, is it? No, don't be upset. It's not you, it's us. We've changed. We really respect you and we like you, we just don't want it to be anything more than that. Okay? Take care, 'bye!*

Maromme's name is boldly displayed on the "Welcome to Oadby" road signs even though most, of my fellow Oadby citizens aren't even aware of the relationship. And though I knew of Maromme, I had no idea what sort of town I would find.

Was I going to be welcome as an envoy? Or was I going to be greeted awkwardly, as someone clumsily trying to rekindle the flames of a romance gone cold?

The visit came about in a peculiar and serendipitous way, the omens bode better than my misgivings on the day itself. My route planning for Walking Home was already pretty advanced when I was checking maps on the internet one day and there it was: Maromme, about four miles north west of Rouen. By an amazing coincidence our twin town was virtually on my walk. I knew immediately I had the chance to turn a Paris to Oadby walk into a twin-towns walk as well.

Our Mayor was very positive when I asked if she would support the visit by writing to her counterpart in Maromme. Debbie, her secretary, sent off a letter in February and we heard nothing for weeks. Even as I was setting off for Paris, we still weren't sure if the appointment would happen but finally, the confirmation came through. We would meet at M. David Lamiray's office at the *Hotel de Ville*, or town hall.

As I came into Maromme, sure enough the road sign made mention of Oadby and Wigston. I grabbed a picture.

The Hotel de Ville is incorporated into a block of residential flats, along with other shops, on one side of a pretty garden. It's an unusual way to arrange things but I quite liked the idea that the administrators of local government work beneath the homes of some of the citizens they serve.

It's not easy to make direct comparisons between French and British systems of local government. British mayors serve for one year in a mainly ceremonial role, opening fêtes, giving speeches at civic events, greeting visiting officials. French mayors, on the other hand, serve an eight or nine year term of office and have considerable executive power.

I arrived at the appointed time but had to wait in a very slow-moving queue at the reception desk. The minutes clicked by on the clock above the receptionist, who was trying to help someone navigate a lengthy form for some planning permit. Eventually, I reached the front of the queue. When I explained that I had an appointment with M. Lamiray, the receptionist made a profuse apology. It confirmed my hunch that the French mayor is someone rather important - a *grande fromage*, as they probably don't say in France. I was directed to the first floor.

The décor was rather swish and I saw M. Lamiray's name on the outside of a padded leather door. I knocked and, when invited to enter, I stepped in. Two men were sitting on either side of a large desk in an impressive office. They looked at me bewildered. I sensed this wasn't going well.

I realised that I had walked through the back-door of the mayor's office, and that I had made a rather novel entrance, in full walking gear.

"Monsieur Lamiray?" I quavered.

The younger of the two men, in an elegant suit, said that yes, he was M. Lamiray. Clearly, I didn't look anything like what he had expected as part of his Monday morning schedule.

Then a moment of recognition flashed on his face. I imagined him thinking, *Mon Dieu, this is the eccentric English walker that I have had to find time for.*

He asked if I would mind introducing myself to his personal assistant, while he finished his meeting.

I apologised and scuttled out. How stupid not to think that a man as powerful as M. Lamiray wouldn't be accessible without negotiating several layers of protective assistants. I breathed deeply. As far as diplomatic *faux pas* go it was minor, unlikely I thought, to result in an 'incident' that would lead to calls from the Embassy. But while there was little chance that I had triggered a series of escalations that would lead to the British fleet sailing up the Seine to the port of Rouen, I winced at the thought that I had represented the citizens of our Borough with the aplomb of Mr Bean.

As I sat in the waiting area outside the mayor's office, where I had been directed by his personal assistant, I noticed the département names on the signs. There was an office for the forthcoming local elections next to me, in which two or three people worked. There were signs to departments for youth, for leisure, for cemeteries, and adoption. It was noticeably quiet, with little chat and very few phone calls. I couldn't imagine that this was the only site for the council, they must have another annexe for all the other staff. Or did French local administration run as a reliable machine, needing the attention of just a few people to keep things ticking along?

M. Lamiray welcomed me into his office and we spent half an hour or so together, the conversation being entirely in French. At one or two moments I wondered if he understood more English than he let on, choosing instead to retain the already considerable diplomatic advantage that I had handed him in my fumbled entrance.

His assured manner and personal presence suggested he was used to exercising real power. He appeared younger than me and I wondered if he was something of a rising star in French politics. He reached across the huge desk for a blank sheet of paper and began to explain the French system of government. A large circle, as wide as the paper, represented France, with its National Assembly, President and Prime Minister. A smaller circle within the larger one represented one of the twenty-six regions, Haute Normandie (Upper Normandy) being the one in which we sat. At this point, M. Lamiray paused and looked me in the eye. He explained that he is a councillor on the regional council.

"Aah!" I gestured in a way that signalled impressed respect, without implying submission. I felt as though I was gaining ground.

M. Lamiray's pen inscribed another, smaller circle to indicate the *département* of Seine-Maritime. France is divided into one hundred numbered départements, which exceed English counties both in their geographical size and in the fierce loyalty of their residents. I had already walked through the departments of Paris (number 75), Hauts de Seine (92), Yvelines (78), Val d'Oise (95), Eure (27). I nodded seriously with a look that tried to suggest, *The departments? But, of course, I know many of them!*

M. Lamiray was enjoying explaining his role and the structures of civil administration to a keen student. The conversation shifted and he asked about my walk, explaining that when the letter first arrived from Oadby and Wigston, already translated into French, he and his staff thought that there must have been some error.

"Could anyone walk from Maromme to Oadby?" he asked in French. "You're not driving? Not going by bus? There's no-one with you?"

The questions tumbled out and I straightened up in my chair, feeling that the diplomatic advantage had shifted now I was playing in a strong suit.

I explained that the route was over eight hundred kilometres and that I had already walked about a fifth of the journey. With a flourish, I pulled the route map from my left trouser pocket (where I kept it throughout the walk for similar demonstrations of my prowess) and pressed home my bid. Now it was my turn to win approving nods and expressions of impressed interest.

Clearly the conversation in my limited French was only going to take us so far, so I asked if I could read my prepared statement. Hugh's translation of the little speech that I had prepared worked out well but when I composed it I had no idea whether I would be delivering it to the mayor alone or whether there would be more people. Following the French news on TV, I had even dreamed one night about addressing a crowd in the style of Nicolas Sarkozy, who makes up for his diminuitive stature with a precise and punchy oratory. Foregoing the president's hubris I pitched instead for a gentle civic formality. I had to trust Hugh, of course, for finding an appropriate tone and for not choosing words which could lead to offence through an inappropriate pronunciation.

Monsieur Mayor, thank you for finding the time to meet with me today. Thank you for your hospitality. (I offered this hopefully, rather than in gratitude, but still wasn't offered a cup of coffee).

I am honoured to be with you and to bring you the greetings of the people of Oadby and Wigston, and of the churches in our Borough. In Oadby and Wigston we are pleased and proud to be twinned with (the beautiful town of) Maromme.

Hugh offered the bracketed description in case the town was stunningly attractive. It wasn't - but I included it anyway, and caught M. Lamiray's surprised eye with a nod to emphasise my appreciation. He returned my compliment with a baffled but grateful look.

I hope that my visit today will assure you that we remember this connection and that the relationship between our towns may be sustained.

May I say a few words about my visit. I am a pastor in the Church of England and minister at the church of St Paul in Oadby. I am taking three months sabbatical in order to pray, reflect and write.

I am walking on a peculiar kind of pilgrimage, from Paris to Oadby, via Maromme. That's 800 kilometres in total. I have walked nearly 200 kilometres already.

I began at the Cathedral of Notre-Dame de Paris, on 23 April, and I hope to be back in Oadby on 12 June. (If you or any of your staff would like to accompany me, you would be most welcome!)

The little joke went down well.

My walk has taken me through La Defense, Nanterre, along the Seine to Vernon, Louviers and Rouen. I have met interesting people and discovered charming places. It has been a great adventure.

I have a card with the address of my website if you are interested to know more.

Please accept this small gift (I reached into my bag and brought out a slim volume of local history of Wigston, kindly sent to me by Jill Gore) *as a token of the friendship of our towns.*

I shall pray for God's blessing on Maromme and all its people as I walk back home to Oadby.

M. Lamiray gave me two guidebooks for the Haute Normandie Region. I was very grateful for them but they were rather huge and heavy. I had already noticed a post office next to the town hall, convenient for me to post the gifts home. It was good to meet and I was glad that our conversation didn't grind to a complete halt due to my lack of French. We exchanged further pleasantries and I was off again.

On the way out of town, I climbed the road that took me into the forest and the spick and span village of Montigny, where I

97

spent the night in the best hotel of the trip so far.

My walking verse for Day Twelve was Psalm 15.1,2: *O Lord, who may abide in your tent? Who may dwell on your hill. Those who walk blamelessly, and do what is right, and speak the truth from their heart...*

I had been pondering verses like this in relation to the tired argument which sets up a false choice between being with God and working for God. I get the message about the dangers of an industrial spirituality where all is exertion and effort, contrasted with the humbler way of sitting in the company of God without trying to earn reward. Of course, Jesus himself pointed to the better way of Mary, who chose to be quietly with him, in contrast to her busy sister Martha, who went about her chores.

But in our day I think the argument slips too easily into an excuse. The joy of Christian spirituality is the way that God chooses to partner with us in his enterprise. The Kingdom of God could be fully established at any time without our help, but it's in the nature of God to share the endeavour with us.

"Walking with God", about which there are more biblical verses than "being with God'", is an altogether more dynamic idea. It suggests that we can go places with the Lord. It reveals the intrinsic purposefulness of life with God, which liberates us from both enslavement and clinging dependence.

The gift of life, the Bible seems to suggest, is not a resource pack to be exploited in the most productive way. Nor is it a gift simply to be held and treasured. It's an adventure to be lived, a journey to be walked, an intrepid expedition.

–

Day Thirteen was as cloudy as the preceding couple of days but began with a drizzle that hung about all morning.

It ended in Caudebec-en-Caux, with me peeling off my socks after an eight-hour, eighteen mile trek over hills which set back the healing of my right leg. A curious pink efflorescence had appeared at the lower part of my shin, warm and sensitive to the touch. This was puzzling, as I didn't think there could be any possibility of infection from an injury which had not broken the skin.

I went to dinner tired and a little miserable, wondering what Sir Ranulph Fiennes would do. The explorer and adventurer has walked alone through deserts, rainforests and across the frozen Arctic. Like the great British heroes of the Victorian era, he seems indestructible. Even when his body reaches its limits, his iron-will sees him through. I remember an interview in which he told how he took his pocket knife to a couple of frost-bitten fingers. Self-amputation, I decided, was not a feasible possibility for me. Even if I had the courage to separate the joint of my knee with a camping fork, knife and spoon set, I wouldn't be going much farther with only half a leg.

There was much in the day's walk that was beautiful and interesting. I had climbed over a thousand feet of ascents in stifling humidity and the tiredness and pain had diminished the thrill that my surroundings deserved from me. There were more forests, with red squirrels, black beetles, a fox hurrying across the road in front of me with a small rabbit in its mouth.

With a mind free of the usual clutter, I've noticed how long-buried stuff has floated to the surface. My head was filled with a tune from my childhood, Percy Dearmer's hymn, *He who would valiant be*. In primary school assemblies I used to wonder what the strange phrases could mean. Long after I left school, and bit by bit, most of the hymn had fallen into place:

He who would valiant be 'gainst all disaster,

Let him in constancy follow the Master.

There's no discouragement shall make him once relent

His first avowed intent to be a pilgrim.

Who so beset him round with dismal stories
Do but themselves confound—his strength the more is.
No foes shall stay his might; though he with giants fight,
He will make good his right to be a pilgrim.

Since, Lord, Thou dost defend us with Thy Spirit,
We know we at the end, shall life inherit.
Then fancies flee away! I'll fear not what men say,
I'll labour night and day to be a pilgrim.

I make no claims to being valiant and my feeble efforts at being a pilgrim have fallen short of John Bunyan's but it was good to refresh my memory with a once-familiar song and to aspire to its vision.

I liked Duclair, a riverside port and home to one of the few remaining *bacs* that ferries cars across the Seine. There wasn't time to stop at the apparently wonderful abbey at St-Wandril, one of the famous abbeys of the Seine that occupy the valley from Rouen all the way to Le Havre.

It was even more concerning that Day Thirteen was the first of three long days before Le Havre. If I felt this sore now, I thought, would I even make it to the coast.

Intrepid explorers were on my mind. I looked up Scott's ill-fated trek across the Antarctic. The part of the legendary story which always makes me pause is the moment when he discovers his team have lost the race to the pole to the Norwegian, Roald Amundsen. And in a way that I couldn't have predicted, the walk of Day Thirteen brought me back to those heroic explorers.

Jean Latham founded a seaplane manufacturing company here in Caudebec-en-Caux after the Great War. In 1928, the company's *Latham 47* was establishing itself as a key aircraft for the French navy. Soon it had an opportunity to prove itself in the most testing of climates, the far north and the Arctic Ocean. The adventure, which was to end in disaster began on the Seine, a little upstream of where I now sat in Caudebec-en-Caux

The Italian polar explorer, Umberto Nobile, had been flying the airship *Italia* across the pack ice north of Spitzbergen, when contact had been lost.

Six weeks later, a *Latham 47* aircraft was tasked with a rescue mission. It took off from the Seine at Caudebec-en-Caux and flew to Bergen, where the pilot picked up the great Amundsen. They flew next day to Tromsö and then set off the following day to find Nobile. They were never heard of again.

In the early nineteen thirties a huge sculpture was carved and set in the cliff above the Seine, which I walked passed. It depicted the *Latham 47* and commemorated the ill-fated mission.

These great explorers are in a different league from me, of course. I wince at the prospect of going to the dentist; they delighted in danger and going into the unknown. And here was I worried about a bruised leg - what a feeble soul I was.

I had arguably the most famous walking verse of all for comfort in this lowest of days. Psalm 23 includes this in the fourth verse: *Even though I walk through the darkest valley, I fear no evil; for you are with me; your rod and your staff - they comfort me.*

The presence of God, that sense of him being with us in the midst of our journey, is not something that is easily described. If a transcendent moment of encounter with the divine, some flash of light had happened on the dark forest paths I could relate it in every detail. It is not so easy, however, to find words to express the plain reassurance that I experienced during the walk, even on a day of anxiety and low mood.

The writer of the psalm speaks of walking, presumably alone, yet knowing God to be with him. The word "with" suggests more to me than the fact of mere presence. It implies that God has made some act of commitment, that he walks alongside and on side. This is a radical move, playing with our notions of God as the one who is permanent, immoveable, unstoppable. In the psalm, it seems to be God who chooses to move, in response to the pace and direction of his human companion. Like a shepherd of the biblical era, he walks behind his flock, looking out for us and sticking with us.

No wonder this is a "comfort" - though this word too needs a little explanation. We tend to think of comfort as warm reassurance, a snuggly, cuddly kind of thing that makes us feel better. But the word has tougher origins. In Latin, *com fortis* implies the giving of strength, lending power. To walk in the company of God is to receive a real strengthening.

So no, I did not receive any mystical experience during my entire walk, no dazzling moment which left me with nothing but a warm glow. Instead as I walked in the knowledge of God's presence, I received a more substantial strengthening of mind, body and spirit.

—

In the morning, I pulled on a sock carefully onto my tender leg. It's condition hadn't changed and I decided that thinking further about it wouldn't help. There were more miles to be walked and I knew I could do at least one more day.

I left Caudebec-en-Caux on the old Havre road, the D982. My thinking was that this would be quiet and a little shorter than staying on the valley floor. French roads are classified by letters: A for autoroutes (the equivalents of our motorways), N for national trunk roads and D for local roads. I had thought that a D road would likely be as quiet as our British B-roads but the D982 certainly wasn't.

I reached it by footpath and walked along the verge as lorries thundered past every few seconds. Being so close to the roaring trucks wasn't particularly frightening but it was bothersome to have to concentrate all the time. To make myself more visible, I used one of the bright orange vests that my friend Sue gave me as a present before I left. I had cut it into two pieces to save weight, fixing one square on the back of my pack and tied to my waistband, dangling like a pennant.

It worked pretty well, though I had tried to remember to fold the dangling bit into my pocket when I reached a pavement on the edge of a town, for the sake of appearance. I had only occasional honks from drivers and mainly in the moments that the terrain forced me to walk on the right side of the road, with the flow of traffic rather than against it.

Before long I had had enough of the D982, so plotted a new course on small country lanes across the limestone plateau of the Pays de Caux, through villages too small for shops or bars. It also led me past a giant sequoia tree at la Guerche. Like me with my orange pennants, it looked incongruous and a long way from home.

I didn't get any lunch until well after two o'clock, when I reached Notre-Dame-de-Gravenchon, a petrochemical town with a peculiar sweet oily smell and hardly anyone around. I must have looked forlorn sitting in the empty market, first munching on a slice of pizza, and then slightly panicky when I realised that I had left my hat on a bench at the other side of the town centre. Fortunately, although half an hour had passed, it was still there. A French refinery town on a bank holiday afternoon has a post-apocalyptic feel to it. I allowed myself to daydream a morbid fantasy. The deserted streets and lingering smells suggested some kind of dreadful disaster, in which a potent toxic gas had worked its way through the place like the Angel of Death. I told myself off for being so ghoulish. All this solitude wasn't doing me good - I looked forward to being in England soon and to proper conversation.

Going further downhill, I was the only pedestrian to walk through the industrial zone, on a road which goes through the centre of the *Exxon Mobil* refinery. The noise of screaming pumps, escaping steam, and blasting fans for the cooling towers filled my ears. The smells ranged from revoltingly sulphurous to pleasantly phenolic. Each installation was a tower of reaction vessels and pipework, with flame-stacks decked around like candles. Some of these produced regular gulps of bright orange flame, some burned with constant brightness, and I saw one whose flame was invisible, its heat betrayed only by the shimmering distortion of the distant chimneys beyond it.

To some, it might all have looked, sounded and smelled infernal. I loved it.

The problem of environmental pollution and our exploitation of the natural world is immense and I wouldn't want to downplay the seriousness of the issues. But to me, the industrial plant I walked through was no more especially symbolic of all that than the hotel room in which I later sat. Most of its fabrics and fittings and even the clothes I wore were manufactured from materials produced in plants like the one at Gravenchon. The industrial machinery is just another link in the chain which produces so much that we all use, together with so many despoiling by-products.

Actually, the petrochemical plants looked quite magnificent. If they suggested human callousness of Creation they might also have suggested human ingenuity. Walking through them I felt as small as I did on the first day of the walk, which took me beneath La Defense's towers of commerce and finance. But unlike those boastful skyscrapers, which try to outshine each other as monuments to corporate ego, the pipes and scaffolds I was now walking among were honestly functional.

I mused on how the money shuffled at La Defense, or Canary Wharf or Manhattan, is really no cleaner than the liquids and gasses that are pumped and churned at Notre-Dame-de-Gravenchon.

I crossed the Seine on a bac ferry to the little town of Quillebeuf-sur-Seine.

The bac was the first form of transport that I've used, apart from my own two feet, since 21 April when Jennifer and I arrived in Paris. Ferries, I decided, were necessarily within my rules, as were lifts and escalators.

The Left Bank of the Seine is very different from the right. It lost out in the competition to receive a railway in the nineteenth century and consequently missed all the investment that followed. I took the quiet road which tracks the riverbank in a sweeping arc, with marshes and quiet farmland to the south. Gradually, more and more grass appeared in the middle of the road and by the time it became a dirt track I felt as isolated from anyone as I had at any point on the walk so far.

I passed under the enormous Pont de Tancarville suspension bridge, built in the nineteen fifties by the Eiffel construction company. By now I was very tired and I hoped that I might find a flight of steps inside the gigantic abutment but I was out of luck. I had to walk another mile away from the river in order to join the road which climbs the approach to the bridge. Two cars came along the quiet road, their drivers looking rather furtive. A little farther along a group of five or six cars were parked alongside a quiet wooded area and I guessed what might be going on. Sure enough, as I passed the cars I realised I was being watched from among the trees, confirming my suspicion that this was a gay cruising venue. A shadowy figure moved among the branches just feet away and I felt I was being checked out. Tired as I was, I picked up the pace.

I had already checked my map which showed one of the *Grande Randonee* long-distance footpaths crossing the bridge. But I was a little surprised at how narrow the pavement was. Once again, I was within a few feet of thundering trucks but this time the road bounced beneath me whenever a full load passed.

At the point where the main suspension cables connected to the deck of the bridge, I had to climb a few steps and walk along a narrow platform to get to the other side. It seemed an odd way to design a route for pedestrians and made me doubt whether it really was open to the public.

Lorry drivers were giving me odd looks and I realised that

At the point where the huge cables joined the decks on the north side, I climbed another little platform to get across. This time, at its far end I had to open a gate to get through and in closing it I noticed its sign: *NO PEDESTRIANS*. If I had seen the sign at the other side what would I have done? Chanced a hitch-hiking lift, possibly with new friends from the cruising site? Or broken down and wept at thought of a further twenty-mile diversion?

I had now crossed the Seine a total of ten and a half times since leaving the island on which Notre-Dame Cathedral sits in Paris.

My walking verse for the day was Psalm 26.3: *For your steadfast love is before my eyes and I walk in faithfulness to you.*

It was a great reminder, on a day which I began in a fed-up mood, to keep my head up, to focus on God's goodness and to simply walk.

The hotel at the foot of the bridge was the only one for some distance. I enjoyed the view across the river and caught sight of a huge container ship sailing past my bedroom window.

The room was very comfortable, as it should have been for the price. Rather mysteriously, a huge red apple sat on a plate, with knife and napkin, as a complimentary welcome gift. It made me wonder how many people reach their room and exclaim with delight, "Ooh look! An apple - how thoughtful!"

It was a treat to have a warm bath and I nervously inspected my leg for signs of further deterioration. Thankfully, marvellously, it seemed slightly better. I had been worried that the sore pinkness was a precursor to weeping ulcers. The long soak gave me opportunity to think about how I could treat it, and I had an idea. The *Ziplock* bags in which I had kept all my gear were strong enough to hold a little water. Sure enough, I found that after filling one with cold water about a third full, the seal would hold. I lay on the bed with a cooling pack on my right ankle.

Eventually it was time for dinner. I descended to the restaurant and looked for the cheapest of the fixed price menus. I had only snacked for lunch and breakfast had been light too, so even though I didn't feel particularly hungry, I knew I needed a decent meal. The cheapest fixed price menu was over thirty Euro - I was only getting an exchange rate of about one pound to the Euro, so this felt very extravagant. I guessed that the hotel was exploiting the fact that there was nowhere else for guests to go without driving.

Oh well. Let's go for it! I thought, reckoning that I deserved a decent meal in consolation for my tiredness and injury. The meal was a lavish affair - clearly the chef was out to impress. I began with a tart of goat's cheese, followed by a selection of cuts of lamb: a tender piece of leg, a chop and two short wooden skewers on which sweetbreads were impaled. It was the first time I had tried the delicacy and though the flavour was more subtle than I thought, I decided to content myself with just a couple of mouthfuls.

—

Day Fifteen began with a death or glory moment. That's an exaggeration, of course, but in my mind solitude was turning things strangely serious. I was faced with a decision which could have had far-reaching consequences for the rest of the walk. The issue was the health of my feet, ankle and legs. Suffering from leg pain in the months before the walk began, I had consulted a podiatrist who made me walk up and down while he looked intently at my gait. He pursed his lips, ducked and leaned to check other angles, and then pronounced his verdict. "You've got serious biomechanical issues."

My feet are flat, it seems. Steve, the podiatrist, explained that the lack of strength in the arches of my feet made me compensate by overpronating. That is, as I completed each stride, I was twisting my foot outwards, so that the last part that left the ground was the inside of my big toe.

"How far are you walking?"

"About five hundred miles."

"You're going to struggle," said Steve, "after a couple of weeks you'll have lots of pain on the outside of your legs beneath the knee: shin splints."

Steve explained that the cure for the problem was to support the arch of each foot. He trimmed little pieces of self-adhesive foam and stuck them to the bottom of the Sorbethane insoles that I was using with my boots.

"Try these. If they help, give me a call and we'll get some proper ones made up for you."

I had rung Steve's department at a nearby hospital to order the orthotic supports but was told that I had left it too late. So I headed off to France with two alternative options, the temporary supports that Steve had fitted to the Sorbethane insoles and some off the shelf gel inserts that I had picked up from a chemist.

I tried the gel inserts for the last two weeks of practice and they seemed alright. But on the walk itself, they had given me blisters within a couple of days. From the third to the fourteenth day of the walk I had switched to the Sorbethane insoles, which were better for my blistered feet but not so good for preventing the leg pain which sure enough, was becoming significant, just as Steve had predicted.

The way forward was an irreversible compromise. I hesitated for a moment, wondering if I was about to commit a reckless act that would jeopardise the whole walk. But in a mood of come what may I took out my knife and began to cut away the worn temporary supports from the Sorbethane.

After a few minutes work, I slipped the gel inserts into my boots and fitted the Sorbethane insoles on top. It felt strange, and I sensed that I had grown taller by half an inch. I had over seventeen miles to cover on Day Fifteen and I hoped and prayed that I would get to the end of the day without making my legs worse.

More choices had to be faced. The day offered two principal alternative routes. Either follow the old main road, the D982 (which I had abandoned the day before for being too busy), or take a walk along the Le Havre/Tancarville canal.

I settled for the latter, crossed the lock which keeps the canal at a constant level whatever the tide, and was soon alone alongside the reeds and marshes. The path was dead straight for three miles and frankly, a bit dull. At first the reeds and birds were interesting but I came to realise how much I had enjoyed walking among people, or at least through places in which there were signs of human activity. My knowledge of wayside fauna and flora is dismal. Months before the walk I had bought a miniature guidebook to European birds but even in the beautifully drawn and annotated drawings they looked uninteresting.

I also felt very alone as I walked and for some reason it mattered more to me than it usually does. Normally content with my own company, this lonely walk felt more like isolation than solitude, if that makes sense. I think I was also a bit fed up with myself. Frustrated at the slow healing of my leg (though thankfully it had looked better when I woke), guilty about the extravagant meal which I hadn't really enjoyed, and nervous about a day's walk that would end in a large and, I feared, unfriendly port.

The narrow track was littered with cattle dung - presumably from the cows in the fields next to me which were occasionally driven along it. The dull character of the road gave me no distraction from my thoughts, which started to explore the dangers of the lonely spot. How likely was it that I would encounter a herd of cattle? How could I avoid them, on a track which offered no shelter between the canal and the steep embankment to the fields? How fresh was that dung?

I looked at it carefully, trying to judge how long it had taken the sun and wind to dry its crust, concluding that it had been deposited within the last day, and that therefore the risk of a cattle confrontation was not insignificant. I told myself off for being stupid, the object of my fear was an imagined threat. I had already come safely through one hundred and fifty miles of walking and I was imagining dangers that weren't real, only anticipated.

This is what walking for two weeks on my own, in a country where I couldn't easily converse with others, was doing to me. I had become a tormented dung-studying fantacist.

After an hour or so, two runners were a welcome sight. They were coming towards me from the huge *Renault* factory at Sandouville and this far from anywhere else, must have been on their lunch break.

I stopped to exchange words with a fisherman. It was great to spend a few minutes chatting. I asked for advice about the best routes and he was very sure that to continue along the canal, past the factories and refineries was dangerous. He told me that I had be better on the main road, which confirmed the decision for me. I thanked him for his salutation of "Bon courage!" and set about crossing the Pont du Hode.

The D982 was lovely and quiet, all the traffic that I had seen on its earlier stretches now being taken by the autoroute, which runs parallel to it. It serves to link the small settlements along the foot of the cliffs and to take the occasional *convoi exceptionnel*, loads too wide or too slow for the motorway.

The D982 turned only where the foot of the cliffs came close to the canal, so for the most part, I walked in straight lines for hour after hour. The rhythm of walking was something I had learned. Easy walking like these flat miles, led me to a kind of relaxed state where I wasn't thinking conscious thoughts. With not much to occupy me, no need to check the map, my mind sometimes wandered but mainly just ticked over. In places and in moods where I sensed danger, as I had along the canal, it was unsettling. But on easy stretches it delivered a pleasant feeling of the world unrolling itself to me.

It didn't even occur to me to put in my earphones to listen to music and I was glad that I decided not to bring my radio. It would have distracted me and filled hours like these with unimportant clutter. Friends had asked me about the music that I would listen to as I walked and were surprised when I said I wasn't going to bring any. Music displaces us, its power to enchant or move us is a problem if we want to engage with our surroundings. Music would have carried me away from France, from the D982, from the moment in which I moved. I would also have lost the beat of the walk itself, in which every step contributed to the percussion.

I had discovered that every person has a preferred tempo for walking and that maintaining the regular cadence of strides is important for walking effectively. This had never occurred to me before, I had simply assumed that I could vary my pace and stride over quite a range. Walking on rough ground involves choosing where to plant a foot, so it's not possible for a consistent rhythm to develop. But after almost two hundred miles on mainly smooth surfaces, I had found a precise pace that suited me. Within half an hour of starting each day, all stiffness had gone and I slipped into the steady walking rythym that lasted all day. When I came to gradients, I had learned not to make each stride more exerting but to reduce its length to maintain the pace. Like a car driver who changes gear when approaching a steep hill, I had found a way to 'shift down'. The miles ticked by.

I did have to keep my wits about me when I came to the motorway junction. I couldn't see any provision for pedestrians so had to stay with the traffic on the flyovers and ramps. The problem with these was that the Armco barrier was right on the edge of the tarmac. Walking behind the Armco was very difficult as the ground was lumpy, littered and overgrown. There was also precious little flat space between the barrier and the steep slope of the embankment, threatening a painful tumble that would have pitched me into the traffic below. Picking a way involved a lot of concentration.

The alternative, on the traffic side of the Armco, was wonderfully smooth and easy going but nerve-wracking. Fully laden loads passed me within a couple of feet and made the bridge bounce.

Having found such poor provision for pedestrians at the motorway junction, within a few miles things changed completely. I was treated to a walk on the same road, this time upon a beautifully surfaced and wide lane, especially reserved for cyclists and walkers. It was at least five metres wide and even had its own posh lamps, bearing the badges of *Total*, the petrochemical company whose site it passed.

Harfleur was for centuries the principal harbour near the mouth of the Seine. As ships grew larger it suffered problems with silting of the deepest channels, so a decision was taken to build a new port at Le Havre. Overtaken by its younger neighbour, Harfleur is now little more than a suburb of Le Havre. I got lost at a complicated road junction, sharing the subways with youths who wore a "What are you looking at?" kind of expression. It turns out that the minor road on my map was now a construction site, so I had to do some backtracking and, for an exciting short stretch, to walk in the traffic on a six-lane dual carriageway with no pavement.

Despite the over-elaborate feast I was served during the previous evening, I had scoffed a large breakfast, knowing that my route to Le Havre didn't promise many shops. I really wasn't hungry by lunchtime, and didn't fancy any of the tiny cafés or bargain stores among the flats on the way in. Instead I picked up a half-baguette and a slice of quiche from a bakers.

Eventually, I got to my cheap hotel and sat down for my supper. On the baguette I spread sachets of jam that I had pilfered from the *Formule 1* hotel breakfast tray a week before, and I poured water into the little plastic cup that was waiting in the room. It was a dramatic come-down from the thirty Euro meal of the day before.

Something strange was happening to my appetite. After the first week of walking, I rarely felt peckish, unlike at home where my tummy rumbles every couple of hours. But when food was before me, I could eat astonishingly huge amounts.

It felt like a significant achievement to reach the French Coast, which was about one-third of my overall distance. I relaxed and allowed myself a little self-congratulation, knowing that three of the hardest back-to-back walks had been accomplished on a dodgy leg. In some ways, my mood and my stamina had been at a low point. I remembered Mark Moxon promising an upturn in fitness in the third week and I was glad that I would be spending the next night on English soil. I had never felt despairing or lonely to the point of wanting to be home - something which I gladly attributed to the divine strengthening about which the psalms had reminded me.

I prayed an even-more earnest thanksgiving when I lay on the bed at the hotel, and thought of the day's walking verse from Psalm 56.13: *For you have delivered my soul from death, and my feet from falling, so that I may walk before God in the light of life.*

I slept for twelve hours.

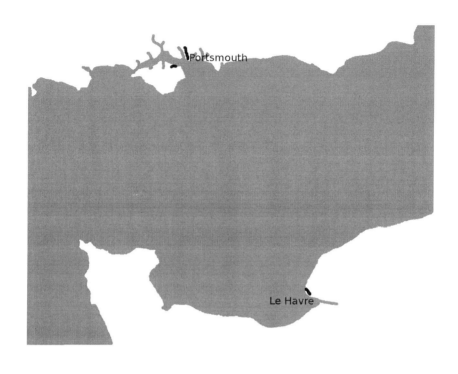

Le Havre to Ryde - just 12 miles of walking, with two ferry journeys

Chapter Four - Le Havre to Ryde

After three hard days, it felt really good to wake up on my last morning in France knowing that time was on my side. Walking days had quickly assumed a routine and there was actually not a lot of time to spare.

I usually woke around seven. For the first half hour I lay in bed, reading any messages or emails that had arrived in the night and thinking about the walk that lay ahead of me. Looking at the maps to make final decisions about the route I had follow took quite a while. I mulled over the paper and lett the towns and contours suggest the kind of day I was in for.

I aimed to finish breakfast by eight-thirty and then it was back to my room to pray and reflect on the previous day. I was much more alert in the morning, my mind not yet numbed by the walking, so this was my best hour for writing the blog.

Eventually I would be ready to pack and go, so after filling my *Platypus* with fresh tap water, I filled the plastic *Ziplock* bags with all my bits and pieces and stashed them in the rucksack. On most days, the socks, shirt and underwear that I had washed during the previous evening had dried thoroughly. But on occasions I had to walk with the socks dangling from my waistband for a couple of hours to get them completely dry.

The packing and leaving always took a frustratingly long time. Some days I got out on the road before ten, on others it was after eleven.

Although I had time to myself in the evenings, I found I was too tired to enjoy them as much as the days. Washing clothes, eating, watching a bit of television and calling home filled the hours before nine thirty, by when I was usually slipping towards sleep.

But Day Sixteen was going to be different. My ferry wasn't due to depart until four o'clock in the afternoon, so I took my time getting ready. Wonderfully, my poor bruised leg looked much better and the soreness was definitely reduced. Eventually, after putting off the cleaners who wanted to get into my room I slipped into a grey, overcast and drizzly Le Havre.

It was actually cold, not just cool. It wasn't the perfect weather to explore a city centre which features more bare concrete than most but I took a perverse pleasure in being an anti-tourist. Le Havre is busy with holidaymakers in the summer months but generally they're passing through. Today, it was eerily quiet.

The eighth of May is a national holiday in France, *Victoire 1945* or, to Brits like me, VE Day. This was the second quiet Friday in as many weeks and the rain conspired to empty the streets even more than the closed shops would have done. I practically bumped into the hideous *Volcan* cultural centre, which looked like an impregnable cooling tower, tilted at an unstable angle. It featured, unaccountably, a huge bronze hand, which held out an open palm from one otherwise bland curved wall. Goodness knows what the architect, Brazilian Oscar Niemeyer, was thinking.

It's easy to be disparaging about modern architecture but I'm keen not to dismiss it out of hand. I had been impressed with

Auguste Perret's church of St Joan in Rouen and Le Havre was a good place to explore more of his work. The city was very badly bombed by the RAF in September 1944 in a series of devastating raids that killed five thousand citizens and destroyed twelve thousand homes. The legacy, apart from untold bereavements and sorrows, is that almost every building in the centre and at the docks was built in the nineteen fifties. Perret was given free rein to create a new Le Havre.

The enormous bell tower of St James' Church loomed over the buildings in the town centre and it was easy to navigate towards it. I was expecting to be disappointed and initially the exterior did nothing to attract me. The octagonal tower rises over one hundred metres and its damp grey concrete matched the tones of the gloomy English Channel and the rain-filled clouds perfectly.

Getting closer though, I saw that the whole height of the tower was studded with thousands of tiny windows.

I was pleased to find the church open for visitors and over the next hour I shared the space with just a handful of tourists. They popped in looked around the darkness and spoke too loud, then left. They probably decided that the bare concrete interior, with no pictures or statues, save for one Madonna and child, didn't hold much more than a moment's interest. But I let the building speak to me on its own terms. In time, my eyes adjusted to the gloomy semi-darkness and I noticed that the thousands of multi-coloured windows were subtly different in shade. In front of me they were mainly yellow and white. To the sides and behind there were darker hues of green and red. The altar stood centrally, beneath a canopy, under the high hollow tower.

To counter the dark grey cavernous space just a hint of natural daylight came in from clear windows at the very top of the tower.

When I was alone, I heard some faint musical sounds, which

I thought at first must be being played in another room. They weren't quite melodic. I wondered if musicians were tuning their instruments in a rehearsal room somewhere. Then I realised the notes were descending from the heights of the hollow tower above me. Barely audible, sustained high string sounds were accompanied by occasional, slightly louder bass chords.

It certainly sounded ethereal, as if the strains of heaven were being beamed down. Gradually I realised that the wind itself was reverberating the structure of the tower and that what I was hearing were the natural resonances of the building in response.

The two-tone horn of a passing ambulance filled the church with sound, which was then spun upwards into the tower. The notes fused together and then fell again in a lingering diminuendo.

I wondered about Perret's intentions and which characteristics of God were emphasised by this remarkable architecture. To me it suggested permanence and immutability - perhaps an emphasis chosen in response to the calamity of war and the devastation all around. The height and brutally bare concrete also implied strength, praiseworthiness, and a masculine kind of lordship. What would it be like to worship here? I thought it would be hard for a community to laugh in this space. But perhaps no one laughed in Le Havre after all that grief.

As I looked around at the empty chairs, I wondered if any of today's congregation remembered the opening of the new church in the late 1950s. I suspected that today's worshippers were few in number as there was little evidence for community life on the notice boards, which only displayed the history of the building and publicity that encouraged vocations to the priesthood.

Perret's vision can't just be dismissed. It felt brave, optimistic and powerful. But perhaps his modernism hoped too much for human achievement, industry and manufacture. It left no room for grace, for playfulness or the peculiar movements of God who comes among us in person.

I walked among the apartment blocks of the UNESCO World Heritage site through more of Perret's concrete block city. It wasn't unattractive, nor was it unkempt or spoilt. It actually looked like a good place to live. But where were the people? Even allowing for the fact it was a chilly bank holiday, there was little sign of anyone out and about, or interacting with each other.

I found my way to the LD Lines ferry terminal building and checked in. In the departure lounge I chatted to a man who was listening to the cricket commentary on a crackly radio. As we watched a huge container vessel enter the docks, I asked him what brought him to Le Havre. "Those," he said, "I drive them for a living."

He explained that when a large ship is one or two days from its destination port the captain has a lot of administration to do and it's common for the vessel to be taken around the coast by a man with local knowledge. He's been "trying to retire" for a long time but can't resist the opportunity to get back onto the bridge when an offer comes in.

On the ferry I met Edward, returning from a job interview in Normandy for a position in the far east. He was leaving for Singapore in two weeks and was determined to use the fortnight for the consumption of as much alcohol as he could find. He found quite a lot during the crossing.

I met a couple now living in Southern Brittany but whose accents were familiar. The woman explained she was from Wolverhampton, so we exchanged stories about my home town.

Due to "adverse tides and winds" we arrived an hour late in Portsmouth. I didn't get out of the immigration building until nearly ten o'clock at night and decided that I would get a taxi to the hotel, instead of walking through Southsea's unfamiliar streets on a dark Friday night. I had wondered whether I would be breaking my self-imposed restriction about not taking transport other than escalators, lifts and ferries. But as I was going to double-back and walk to the port for the trip to the Isle of Wight the next day, I decided that I derived no real advantage from the ride apart from safety. Besides, they were my rules.

My walking verse for the day was from Psalm 82.5: *They have neither knowledge nor understanding, they walk around in darkness.*

I reckoned that I had little knowledge or understanding this particular hard-drinking port on a Friday night. I didn't fancy walking around in darkness either!

The Ferryman Guest House was excellent. Furnished in a comfortable nineteen thirties style, it allowed me a lovely night's rest. James, the landlord, greeted me the following morning with words that I had been longing to hear: "Would you like a full cooked English breakfast?"

–

Breakfast at The Ferryman Guest House was served on the top floor, and in some style too. James has furnished The Ferryman in a manner consistent with the thirties era of the building itself, and I enjoyed my delicious cooked English breakfast in black and white surroundings. Fried food made a wonderful change from bread and jam. But what was really tremendous was sitting in a room with other people, being able to join conversations or at least to overhear them. The isolation caused by my poor French language skills was over. After two and a half weeks on my own I learned just what a blessing it is to be able to converse and to connect.

This was the sort of insight that I was hoping for in my adventure. I'm naturally something of an introvert; I love to be involved with people but quite content to be on my own. Part of the joy of being a vicar is to be around people much of the time. A typical week will include long conversations about the deepest things, but also many meetings and casual chats. It's a real treat to have time to myself.

At *The Ferryman*, I realised how much I need to be with other people. During the previous week the isolation had somehow intensified and I knew my mood had fallen. The walk had never felt bleak and I had still been enjoying it but I realised how much I needed company.

In the breakfast room I was joined by a man, of about the same age as me, and his seven or eight year old son. We got talking about what brought us to Southsea. He told me that he only has access to his son on alternate Saturdays and that this trip was a treat for them both. It was moving to see them interact. They took special care of each other in the way they talked about the food and about what they might do together. This time, I realised, was so precious to them both. And of course, I thought about Jon and Phil, my sons whom I hadn't seen for over two weeks.

A young French woman came and sat at another table. James asked her how her performance went. When he saw my eavesdropping, he explained that she was a pianist who came to give a recital. Her English was far better than my French but she still looked nervous. She gave an equivocal answer to the question about the recital and uncertain responses to the offer of the various components about a regular cooked English breakfast. I saw in her the same quivering apprehension that I had lived with in France. The comparison revealed how much *at home* I now felt.

Set up for the day, I walked back to the port and chanced upon a block of flats bearing a plaque. It recorded that the flats stood on the site of earlier houses in which Arthur Conan Doyle lived and practised as a local doctor, and that the first two *Sherlock Holmes* stories were written there.

A little farther on, I found the City Museum and a whole

exhibition on Conan Doyle and the *Holmes* phenomenon. It also explored Doyle's bizarre beliefs and his interest in spiritualism which dominated his later life. He was one of the leaders of the fashionable fascination in spiritualism which followed the Great War. (Before the day was out, though, I was to end up in even stranger quasi-religious territory, in the town in which the self-proclaimed Son of God now lives and writes about the reptilian super-race that apparently rules the earth.)

I really didn't know what to expect from Portsmouth, only having driven through it to the cross-channel ferries before now. It was a great place - bustling with crowds brought out by warm Saturday sunshine. Gunwharf Quay led to the Spinnaker Tower, whose lift sped me skywards by over one hundred metres. This had to be one of the most spectacular panoramas I have seen. From Southsea to the Isle of Wight, Gosport and the naval dockyard, there was such a lot to look at. I watched an American naval vessel come into port and tie up among the British frigates and destroyers. In the water beneath my feet, heavy ferries danced around the tiny yachts with a daring impatience.

A chocolate-smooth pint of *Abbot Ale* slipped down very easily outside the *Ship Anson* pub, while morris dancers entertained the crowds on the quay. My first day in England - fried breakfast, *Sherlock Holmes*, real ale and morris dancers. How stereotypical!

A one-way ticket on the catamaran ferry to Ryde on the Isle of Wight cost me £10.80 for an eighteen minute ride, which I thought was extortionate. We docked and walked along the tatty pier into the once highly-fashionable resort. Ryde boasts some splendid Edwardian homes but my budget guest house was among the more modest buildings.

After a short walk to find a church in which to worship the next morning, I looked for somewhere to eat. The nearby Indian

restaurant declared that they were fully book, even though I would have been their only customer. Grumpy about the rejection, I walked on and found a restaurant whose chairs were vinyl-covered pads resting on the same welded frames that supported the melamine table-tops. Cod, chips and peas and my first mug of tea for three weeks, all for less than a fiver.

It was all so different from France, which already felt like an adventure from long before. I fell asleep to sounds I had not heard for a while; the drunken screams and shouts of British youth at play.

My walking verse for the day was Psalm 115.7: *False idols have hands but do not feel; feet, but do not walk; they make no sound in their throats.*

Human beings have an innate need and capacity to worship, to give themselves to something exterior. Even most atheists agree with this fact. Arguments against the existence of God often include the idea that all religion is the worship of human inventions, the projection of our longings and fears onto a contrived god or a set of gods. All this, so the argument goes, is a mere displacement or, worse, a kind of disempowering exploitation which renders people into dependency. Ironic then, that the Jewish Scriptures (our Old Testament) name and condemn this very kind of enslaving idolatry.

Our appetite for worship, just like our other appetites, can be misdirected in harmful ways. Worship, of course, needn't involve anything that looks like religion. The careerist who neglects family, friends and colleagues in order to fulfil his ambition has worshipped the idol of success. Others devote themselves to wealth or possessions. Still more to fame and celebrity.

Worship is a risky business, always involving a yielding of the self to that which is considered ultimate. It always involves sacrifice. We should be careful what we worship.

The God of the Hebrew Bible resists being tamed and domesticated. "He" (though this gender-specific pronoun is too limiting) is always beyond. He is always *other*. Yet he may be encountered and, at times, approached. In Jesus Christ, Christians believe that this same God is revealed to us in an accessible way. In getting to know Jesus, following him and trusting ourselves to him, we can enter into a full relationship with the divine author of all being.

Yet there is, and always was, a market for more convenient versions of God. The idols mocked for their inability to walk were statues of gods. The psalm-writer is teasing people for trusting in an inanimate object, for putting their superstitious hope in something less than the real untameable God.

Mute and lame idols have certain advantages as objects of worship. Pocket-sized or conveniently static, they can be implored at will to serve the ends of the hands that made them. Idols appear to lend back the power invested in them to their human owners and handlers.

Conan Doyle's brilliant creative powers led him to imagine all sorts of weird aspects of the spirit-world and he convinced himself into a very strange world-view before he died (or, as he would have preferred, "passed on").

David Icke is the Leicester-born one time Coventry City goalkeeper, BBC reporter and Green Party spokesperson who made his own extraordinary and rather sad journey into mystic self-deception in the nineteen eighties. He now lives in the town where I was staying for the night. In Ryde he has written over forty books, claiming that he has specially-revealed knowledge about the shadowy conspiracy which he claims rules the word, at the behest of alien overlords. This is a modern-day *gnosticism*, promising a route to salvation, health and happiness through the acquisition of hidden knowledge. There is, of course, a huge market for both gnosticism and idolatry. They offer a deal, a bargain - salvation for a price. Have some loose change in your pocket, or a tidy sum in your bank account? Then you have the power to buy yourself salvation. This grasping for God, or something that might be a substitute for God, is all around us. In the guise of spiritual quest, it might even infect pilgrims who are hoping to attain some betterment of themselves.

Worship of the one true God, on the other hand, entails a frank recognition of our own smallness and poverty, of ourselves as creatures, not creators. Worship is essentially an act of service, of giving, not acquisition. Yet (and this is the wonderful paradox) grown-up worship does not ultimately diminish us. It dignifies us with the fact that we are unnecessarily and lavishly beloved of God. Even as we worship him, we are borne up by him.

I was discovering afresh that simply walking before God without shrine, statue, or altar, without clerical role or robes, without St Christopher's medallion or lucky charm can be a little step along that road.

–

It's always fun to go to another church incognito. Walk in wearing a clerical collar and I am treated quite differently, usually with an annoying deference. It's much better to see things through the eyes of a visitor. Sometimes I am impressed by the welcome and interest I receive. Sadly more often I feel let down by churches that don't seem very concerned about someone coming in for the first time.

St James was the third Anglican church I had considered that morning. I had initially planned on the church that I had walked past on Saturday evening, but Diana the landlady told me over a rather plain breakfast that I would be fortunate to be in a congregation of more than six. After so long on my own, I really wanted to join a crowd.

I set off and visited the biggest church in Ryde, whose impressive building stands behind a wall on a neatly trimmed lawn, on a road of huge houses. Everything was "proper" but it was curious to spot the word "traditional" twice on the noticeboard. It was an emphasis I wasn't looking for on this particular day. I found another church.

I was welcomed at the door of St James' with a handshake and a smile. There was further genuine welcome from the man who gave me a hymn book and notice sheet, and an easy conversation with a lady who asked if she could join me in the box-pew. When incognito, I don't pretend that I am not a vicar. It's just something I don't advertise. So when asked if I was staying in Ryde for a holiday, I truthfully replied that I was just passing through on a long walk. After the service, a man came up to me and started a friendly chat. It was an excellent example of the vital informal ministry of making people welcome and I was thankful for all the hospitality I received.

St James is an unusual church in the Church of England. There were no signs that it is an Anglican church, and at times in the service I wondered if it was completely independent. The minister wore suit and tie and preached from the central lectern, with no sign of communion table nor candles. He told me afterwards that it's a peculiar kind of *extra-parochial* church, adding, rather gleefully, that his congregation pays no parish share. (The parish share is the collected income for the provision of ministry across a Diocese. The system aims to balance need and the ability to pay, so that clergy are all paid the same and are not deployed to those who pay the most. When it works well, it's a good way of sharing the responsibility of supporting churches in poorer areas).

The style was "conservative evangelical", with a sermon on John 3.36 that focussed on substitutionary atonement and, according to the minister, the simplicity of the implications of acceptance or rejection of Christ. "It's not rocket science!" he said.

It was orthodox stuff, albeit rather un-nuanced, and preached with skill and conviction. The congregation was a similar size to my own St Paul's, but with a greater proportion of children and teenagers.

I was invited to join the church for coffee afterwards and it was good to be among them. Word got around from the nice man that came to chat with me that I was on a long walk and I eventually revealed to one or two (but not the minister) what I normally do. I shuffled out and into the fresh wind that was blowing up from The Solent.

After watching Jenson Button win the Spanish Grand Prix, I set off for another walk along the coast east of Ryde. It was odd to be walking on a "non-walking day" and without a pack on my back I experienced a curious floaty feeling. It was almost like being back on the rolling ferry.

I began the stroll in a bit of a fed-up sort of mood. Without a proper journey to make and with time to kill, I was missing Jennifer, Jon and Phil more than ever. Being at the seaside, among families and couples, reminded me even more of who wasn't with me. And The Solent, with mainland Britain so close but so apparently separate, made me feel more distant than I had felt in France.

Soon the cool wind dropped and as I walked I felt a familiar rhythm return. I strolled through a park in which a great gang of children were playing war games. They divided into "English" and "German" sides, just as I did forty years before. Their grandparents may not even have been alive during the war, yet here they were, taking national sides in an acted-out conflict. These social memories run deep. They played a clear-cut goodies-and-baddies kind of war game and I thought of the confusions of a bombed-out Le Havre in the summer of 1944.

By the time I stopped and sat on a bench, the wind had fallen completely and through the high clouds the sun was lovely and warm.

Proverbs 4.12 was today's walking verse: *When you walk, your step will not be hampered; and if you run, you will not stumble.*

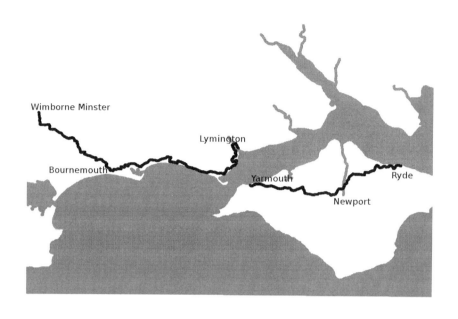

Ryde to Wimborne Minster - 48 miles of coasts, seaside towns and quiet country

Chapter Five - Ryde to Wimborne Minster

It's funny , I thought to myself over a cup of coffee in a seaside cafe, how I was bumping into things. (This, you will understand, was a metaphor for a walk that was full of coincidences, rather than perpetual collisions.)

For example, without my knowledge the Isle of Wight was in the middle of a walking festival, which accounted for the numbers of booted and anorakked walkers that filled Ryde (more than I could have shaken a *Leki* walking pole at). At the climax of the festival over eleven thousand people would "Walk the Wight" in aid of the island's hospice. The full route is a tough twenty-seven miles.

Within minutes of leaving Ryde on the Coastal Path, I had seen more walkers than during the whole of my one hundred and seventy five miles in France..

The path took me to Binstead where Nick, a friend from Bristol days is vicar. We had arranged to meet but a few weeks before I set off for Paris Nick had to change his holiday plans. He was still in a Mediterranean resort while I stood in the porch of his church, reading his parish weekly newsletter.

Nick and I met during my placement in the inner-city parish of Barton Hill, as part of the *Urban Theology Project* that I undertook. Binstead couldn't have been more different from Barton Hill, with gorgeous views through the trees to the sea and thatched cottages next to the church.

Back in those Barton Hill days, the parish had begun to benefit from the first wave of ten-year *New Deal for Communities* regeneration schemes. At the time it was hard to see how people were thinking creatively about using the ten million pound programme beyond improvements to litter bins and street lights. I was looking forward to returning as part of my walk to discover what impact had been made. It was good material for reflection in the light of today's walking verse, Proverbs 8.20: *I, Wisdom, walk in the way of righteousness, along the paths of justice.*

It made me wonder where the "paths of justice" lay in our day. I reckoned that unlike the coastal path of Wight they are unlikely to be mapped on convenient leaflets. Perhaps one always has to ask for directions to stay on the paths of justice.

It wasn't much farther along the path to the old abbey at Quarr, and then past its more modern replacement. Having resisted the invitation to coffee given on the abbey's noticeboard, I paused for a refreshingly-hoppy half-pint of Goddard's bitter at *The Fishbourne Inn*.

After crossing the creek into Wootton Bridge, I picked up the old railway line and pottered among the trees towards Newport. It was a fabulous day for walking westwards - bright sunshine in a clear sky but with a strong east wind behind me that kept me cool.

The wind creaked the trees and at one point I stopped on the track as I heard branches falling. Within a moment of me stopping, a small bough landed on the path in front of me. What were the odds of me being felled by a heavy tree, I wondered.

The OS 1:50,000 *Landranger* series of maps took some getting used to after plotting courses on the French IGN series for so long. I also missed the French system of marking footpaths with coloured blazes painted on the tree trunks, walls or telegraph poles. What first felt haphazard back in the outskirts of Paris had been very effective. There was no moment in France in which I wondered which way to go. By comparison, the British system of using expensive (and therefore occasional) signposts left more room for uncertainty.

I should also mention that in France, not once did a path take me through fields of cattle, nor through farmyards stalked by prowling, untethered dogs. I had come to the conclusion that country footpath-walking in France is an altogether easier and less stressful experience than in England.

I realised that the OS map had deceived me when I couldn't get across a dilapidated bridge. The map showed a row of green dots to indicate a cycle route along the old railway but I discovered that I needed to rejoin the main road for a mile and then pick up the old track again.

The Newport *Travelodge* looked very new and clean and I realised once again how tatty I must have looked at the end of a day's hike.

"Have you made an early check-in reservation?"

"No," I replied, glancing at my watch. It was two-thirty in the afternoon. "Is that a problem?"

The young woman told me with a smile that there was no problem. "But if you want to get into your room before three, you have to pay a little extra."

"How much extra?"

"That will be ten pounds."

I coughed. "Ten pounds? For half an hour in my room?"

She gave me a look of friendly sympathy mingled with a

firm loyalty to the corporate code. I pictured my room, all clean and ready for me, but at ten pounds for the half-hour, more expensive than any hotel room I had ever stayed in. That's a rate of five hundred pounds a day!

"In that case, can I leave my bag here while I go for a coffee in the town?"

"Sorry sir, that won't be possible."

I cleared my throat. "I tell you what," I said in a way that I hoped repaid her firm and friendly tone, "I'm going to sit right here until that clock says three."

Fuming self-righteously, I hoped that my untidy appearance made the Travelodge reception look cluttered. For a few minutes, I regretted the decision to stay in an anonymously corporate hotel.

Then the receptionist came across.

"I can make you a coffee," she smiled. "It's complimentary."

I smiled back. She'd won me round.

The bedroom was simply wonderful. My previous two nights at the bed and breakfast in Ryde were in a rather dull and depressing room. I took it all back now, I loved the anonymous and corporate *Travelodge*. The room was huge, the shower perfect, the flat screen television just right. How shallow I am.

Sue and I met a decade earlier, when we were both ordained at Lichfield Cathedral. She'd served a curacy not far from me and we'd met up quite a lot during our training. But we'd gone our separate ways, me to Leicestershire and Sue to Newport, as prison chaplain. She was the first person I was going to meet on the walk in a kind of reunion.

We met at the hotel and walked with her friend to *The Castle Inn*. The crab-cakes and sautéed potatoes were scrummy, as were the pints of Goddard's *Castle Ale*, brewed especially for the pub, that helped them down. The Castle claimed to be the oldest pub in

Newport and that King Charles I used to visit the pub, under armed guard, whilst he was held prisoner in Carisbrooke Castle. It was also apparently the last pub in England to be licensed by Parliament for cock-fighting, in 1705.

Sue helped me understand a little more of what she called "island mentality". It involved a treasured identity and rather guarded outlook and I sensed that those born on the island have a certain knowing attitude to visitors and newcomers. But Sue, a metropolitan soul if ever there was one, says that the isolation brought by the three-mile wide Solent had eroded even her outgoing spirit.

"After five years here, everything's become small. It creeps up on you, so that you hear yourself saying about a ten mile journey, *'but that's the other side of the island!'"*

–

It was funny how quickly the novelty of a full cooked breakfast wore off. After the lovely meal the previous evening, I didn't really want to kick off Day Twenty with a full fry-up. So foregoing the all-you-can-eat Travelodge breakfast buffet (for a supplementary charge) I popped round the corner to a café.

Newport is the island's administrative centre. But its entire population is smaller than that of the suburban parish in which I live. Oadby is a town which tries to pretend it's still a village. Newport is a village with civic offices and national chains of shops.

I enjoyed the little museum in the Guild Hall, good value for £2. The first floor gallery was being prepared for opening. At the time of my visit, the ground floor displays took visitors through pre-history Wight (lots of fossils) and the Anglo-Saxon era but not much else. It therefore presents a kind of history familiar to children who have studied the schools national curriculum, an uneven pattern of intensely-studied selected periods and not much overall narrative to hold it together. Still, the Anglo-Saxon stuff was pretty impressive, particularly the bronze skillet which is believed to have been for spooning water over babies at their baptism.

In places, Newport didn't appear very keen to show itself to visitors in a particularly attractive light. I had become a student of municipal public seating, developing a keen personal interest in nice places to rest my weary legs. I had discovered that even the smallest of French towns has seats, usually outside the town hall and sometimes along their wider streets.

Someone in Newport once thought that it would be a good idea to make a resting spot outside the county council offices. Judging the architectural style, I conjectured that the idea occurred sometime in 1971 and following construction was neglected from early 1972.

Bench seats had been set into a curved wall around two flower beds, each of about two metres across. One featured an enormous, flower-less, overgrown shrub. The other was bare mud. All of this just yards from the county council offices where someone probably has responsibility for the urban environment. I sat under the gaze of the CCTV camera (another British urban ornament that hadn't featured in France) and noticed the tired-looking Newportians.

The town was still coming to terms with the loss of six hundred jobs announced by the factory that manufactures wind turbine blades. This surprised me - I thought that business would be booming. But it seems that across the United Kingdom, our wretchedly slow planning process had left the wind turbine industry becalmed. Production was being transferred to more positive markets overseas where the winds of state-supported innovation were blowing more reliably.

I left Newport after dining on a coronation chicken baguette, scoffed as I marched along the Carisbrooke Road. The twelfth-century St Mary's Church at Carisbrooke looked like it was made of apple-crumble, its stone having been pitted and worn by eight centuries of wind and rain. I tried the door. It was open and a lovely treat lay inside. The wooden Commonwealth-era pulpit is a rare example of its kind and I wondered who had preached God's word from it ever since 1658. I crept up and stood in it for a few moments, letting my imagination populate the empty pews with stern but godly parishioners.

I took a country footpath, joined the A3054 at Lower Watchingwell and followed it through spots of rain into Shalfleet, where the *New Inn* delivered me a satisfyingly malty pint of amber-coloured beer, whose name I forgot to note.

Jayne at *Northmead Bed and Breakfast* in Bouldnor made me very welcome. Not only did I have Radio Four to listen to for the first time in over three weeks but there was even a green foil-wrapped *Viscount* biscuit waiting for me. Perfect.

By the time I'd showered, the weather was turning worse, so I decided to stay in and dine modestly. I unwrapped a flapjack for dinner.

My walking verse for the day was Proverbs 9.6: *Lay aside immaturity, and live, and walk in the way of insight.*

Blogging my journey had been fun. I was also posting to *Twitter* and *Facebook*. By nature, these forms of communication are chirpy and trivial. I wondered, not for the first time, how the jolly banter of these social networks, related to the call for maturity in verses like the one for this day.

I had read during the previous week that I had featured in a list of the top ten "twittering bishops and clergy". I wondered what it meant for me and my ministry. There was scarcely any time for proper editing of the blog and I was conscious that with a careless word I could embarrass myself, or worse, the church. Months before I set off, I had blogged a note about my newly acquired walking underwear. A member of my congregation sent me an anxious email, protesting that I had revealed too much information. The unnerved parishioner said that they wanted their clergy to preserve an air of mystery, and "to be rather like the royal family".

It was a troubling moment. I certainly didn't want to cause offence, and didn't think what I had written would do so. It made me wonder whether I should be blogging at all. If I wrote inoffensive and rather "worthy" pieces, they may not be very interesting to anyone. On the other hand, I wasn't trying to become a celebrity.

It would have been safest to keep quiet and avoid any risk at all. But I wondered if *walking in the way of insight,* as the Proverb has it, could involve fresh forms of communication in attractive ways.

–

After a few days of shorter walks it felt good to be making steady progress again. In the mornings I was now feeling hardly any stiffness. My blisters and bruises had healed and I was thankful to be feeling quite fit. Within an hour of hauling on my backpack each day I picked up the walking rhythm again and by lunchtime I was practically bouncing along.

Jayne, my landlady, served me a nice breakfast in my room and I set off on the coldest day of my journey so far. It was overcast and there were spots of rain in the air.

After Ryde and Newport, which each had their disappointments, Yarmouth was a delight. It was much smaller, less developed and largely free of traffic, partly due to the closure of the Yar bridge for over a year.

I could have taken the ferry to the mainland immediately but instead pottered about the little harbour, examined the splendid lifeboat and had a pot of tea at the *Marine Café*, which featured an enormous ice-cream machine of the type I remembered from my childhood. Before ducking into the café, I had first picked up a paper from the nearby newsagent, as hitherto my experience of complimentary reading material in the island's cafés has been two *Daily Mails* and one *Hello* magazine. Wight is that kind of island.

My favourite Yarmouth story concerns Sir Robert Holmes, a seventeenth century admiral who raided the French fleet from his base in the town's harbour. On one particularly successful operation, he captured a French ship. Among its crew and cargo he found a craftsman in the process of carving a grand statue of King Louis XIV. The sculptor's work was well-advanced but the head was unfinished. Sir Robert saw an opportunity and insisted that the man complete the piece but with a modification. He demanded that his own head should be carved instead of the French monarch's. It stands as a memorial to Sir Robert in St. James's Church today.

I sat on the "sun deck" for the ferry trip through murk, mist and light drizzle to Lymington, whose pubs and cafés were considerably more expensive than on the island.

In *The Ship Inn*, full of lunching ladies, I chose a glass of *Aspall's Suffolk* light and sharp cider to accompany my game and cranberry pie with mustard mash, carrots and beans.

I walked past Lymington's marinas and out onto its coastal sea defences, past The Salterns where for centuries after the Norman conquest salt was gathered. A series of lagoons were flooded with seawater and then sealed so that, by a process of evaporation, the salt could be concentrated and collected. The Salterns also appeared to be the dog-walking capital of southern England.

At Keyhaven I joined the road again, passing a sign which read "CAUTION - OTTERS CROSSING" and made my way to Milford-on-Sea. The funeral parlour stands opposite a beauty salon by the name of *Drop Dead Gorgeous*. I gleefully noted that the splendid *Baytrees B&B* boasted a four star award from the English Tourist Board, and I was greeted with a tray of complimentary goodies - chocolates, biscuits, bottled water, and a decanter of sherry (which remained un-poured). By far the best feature for me was the room's huge en-suite bathroom, with a bath deep enough to wallow in up to my neck.

My walking verse for the day was Proverbs 20.7: *The righteous walk in integrity - happy are the children who follow them!*

–

Breakfast at *Baytrees* was a splendid way to begin the third week of the walk. After coffee, juice, toast and cereal I opted for the smoked haddock and poached eggs. I was finding that I could pack away a good deal at the meal table but even I had a challenge with this. But since perseverance had become my watchword, I stuck my task and every deliciously smoky, fishy, eggy mouthful eventually disappeared.

The day began brighter than I had predicted and I walked under an overcast sky in mild tee-shirt weather. Only as I reached the cliff path on the coast did the first specks of rain start to fall.

For the long-distance walker, the decision about when to get out the wet-weather gear is a tricky one. As the drops fell, I kept looking to the sky and trying to decide if the rain would persist.

Half-an-hour's light drizzle wasn't much to worry about; the dampness dries almost as fast as the rain falls. But if the drizzle turned to steady rain, or continued for an hour or more, my legs and my backpack would just get wetter and wetter.

I made the call. It wasn't going to get any worse. And with a fresh breeze blowing off the misty sea, I continued westwards in dry-weather gear.

The cliff-top path would be spectacular on a clear day. As it was, I had to peer through the gloom to make out The Needles on the western end of the Isle of Wight.

The coastline here is eroding badly. The path is dotted with warning notices but they're superfluous. It's obvious that the soft soil at the edge of the cliff is subsiding regularly. I didn't want to walk any closer to the edge than the deep cracks in the turf-covered soil.

At Barton-on-Sea I had to leave the cliffs as the footpath was closed due to "unstable ground conditions". That was a pity, as it would be the last stretch of out-of-town walking that I would tackle for a few days.

I turned inland and got lost on a modern housing estate. The twisty roads made it hard to keep my bearings and the thick cloud meant I couldn't get clues from the position of the sun. For the first time in over two hundred miles, I tugged on the red string behind my back and retrieved the compass from one of my rucksack's side pockets. I drew curious glances from locals in the suburban side street as I stood there, map and compass in hand, under a waterproof hat, shrouded in coat and rucksack.

The wise have eyes in their head, writes the Teacher in Ecclesiastes 2.14, *but fools walk in darkness. Yet I perceived that the same fate befalls them all.*

Hmm. True enough. Uncertain as to which of these two categories I belonged to, and frustrated by the obscurity of my route, I found my way through the twists and turns onto the main road.

During another bus-shelter lunch of flapjack and water the rain began to fall with increased intensity. I had congratulated myself on making the right decision earlier and now wondered if it really was time to don the full wet-weather gear. With another four hours to go, I thought it probably was. It turned out to be another good call.

On came the waterproof over-trousers and the silver rucksack cover, which turned me into something like an astronaut from a cheap nineteen-fifties science fiction film. To be a long-distance urban walker, you don't have to mind what you look like.

Highcliffe was quite an upmarket spot, with stylish shops and, judging from the way people dressed, with a significant amount of money. The hotels and B&Bs all boasted awards and looked very fancy. They're out of my league, I thought. The town was a Victorian resort and had re-branded itself at least twice. Before the charming "Highcliffe" it bore the rather uninspiring "Newtown" and before that its original name, "Slop Pond". No wonder they changed it.

Passing through Friar's Cliff I approached Christchurch, skirting Muddeford and Stanpit. As I had only paused for a few minutes at lunchtime, I thought I deserved a sit down and that a nice dry pub would be welcome. I chose the *Ship in Distress*.

Clambering out of the waterproofs was a nuisance but worth it, I supposed, for a comfortable rest-stop and a swift half-pint. Nothing at the *Ship in Distress* was very swift that afternoon, however.

A woman appeared behind the bar, glanced at me, then disappeared again. She re-emerged ten minutes later and snapped grumpily, "You'll have to wait."

I stood and waited another ten minutes.

By now I had concluded that the pub was neither interested in my custom, nor deserving of it, so I hauled on the gear again and left in a bad mood.

In the centre of Christchurch I found the *Olde George Inn*, and sat with a half-pint of *Dorset Piddle*. The pub had some charm but the atmosphere was tainted by the landlady's tuneless singing in accompaniment to the jukebox. She belted out Chris Rea's, "This is the road to hell." Quite so, I thought.

I would have liked longer to explore the Priory and the museums but time was pressing and the weather showed no sign of improvement. A gang of schoolboys huddled around the tailgate of a sweet lorry, in a scene that looked like a re-enactment of a nineteen sixties comic.

"Got any gob stoppers, mister?" I expected them to say. Perhaps if they did they would have had their ears cuffed by the driver for drooling into his boxes of liquorice sherbets.

I muddled my way through the back streets and out into Southbourne, West Southbourne, Pokesdown and Kings Park. Dodging under the pedestrian subway I emerged into

Bournemouth's lovely Queen's Park. Once again I had to get the compass out to make sure I was going to emerge on the north side of the golf course.

I reached Jenny and Chas's house at five-forty, just as I had predicted. It was great to see them and really good to be in a home that I knew. It made me realise that for over three weeks I had nothing familiar around me, save for the gear that I had carried.

We've known each other for twenty three years. Jenny and Chas were engaged when they joined the church at Heath Town in Wolverhampton. Soon after, we saw them marry and we became friends. We spent a lot of time at each other's homes, talking politics and Christianity late into the night. They were the kind of conversations which ranged across the topics until we found something to disagree about. Then for hours we'd pick over the details, getting more and more agitated until we realised that we basically agreed after all. We've spent many holidays together, been godparents to each others children, shared in each others many highs and a few lows. Ours is the sort of friendship that needs no special arrangement each time we meet. We simply get on with it.

–

I now had two days rest. Jenny enlisted me to help assemble props for her church service on Sunday morning. This involved dismantling and cleaning a giant outdoor construction set, before re-assembling it into something that could represent the walls of the city of Jerusalem, for a dramatic re-telling of the story of Nehemiah.

I helped Jenny with the Christian Aid house to house collection that was taking place across the country. It felt odd to be out on the streets for a different purpose, knocking on doors rather than walking past them. I put my winning smile to the test, each time a door was opened.

My previous experience, especially in disadvantaged parishes, is that almost all people give something. But here in these affluent homes, the response was dismal.

"Hi! I've come to collect the Christian Aid charity envelope that was put through your door a few days ago."

"No, thank you."

Time after time I was rebuffed with a firm, slightly awkward rejection. I wondered if I was off-putting in my manner of greeting, so varied the approach.

"Good evening, I'm collecting on behalf of Christian Aid. Would you like to make a donation?"

This was, if anything, even worse. In asking a question, I had made it even easier to receive a refusal.

I tried to subdue the irritation which I felt inside. Never have I received such a miserly response. In poor districts, it's usual for three-quarters of people to give something. Here in this uncharitable part of Bournemouth, no more than one in four gave anything. I felt like shaking the town's dust from my feet.

This frustration was soon forgotten as Jennifer and Phil arrived. We were reunited for the first time since Paris, three weeks before. It was great to change into non-walking clothes and to talk into the late night about all that had happened to us. Phil was preparing for AS exams in the middle summer of his sixth-form while Jon, a year ahead, was about to take his final A2 exams. I was concerned that not being around would be unhelpful for them both and despite talking on the phone most days, it continued to bother me throughout the walk that I wasn't there for them.

One of the blessings of my close friends and my loving family is the way that they keep my foot on the ground. Teasing has always been part of the banter we've enjoyed with Jenny and Chas, and plenty came my way during my stay. I guess my many foibles invite the gentle mocking that I take as a sign of love.

My walking verse was also delightfully humbling, lest I should think that making an epic journey should make me special. In Ecclesiastes 10.3, a judgement is pronounced: *Even when fools walk on the road, they lack sense, and show everyone that they are fools.*

–

On Saturday, Jennifer and I pottered about, went to the local shopping centre to buy, among other things, a replacement for the rather girly-looking timepiece that I had bought in France when the strap on my watch broke.

There are no great stories to tell of Day Twenty Four, just of an ordinary family doing ordinary family things together - it felt like a real treat.

By lunchtime, Jon had driven down to meet us, and the Harvey family were reunited again. We went for a walk to a windswept Hengistbury Head and ate out at a Chinese restaurant. Jon made the long trip back to Leicester in the evening, taking Phil home with him.

My walking verse for the day was Isaiah 2.5: *O come, let us walk in the light of the Lord!*

–

I woke early so that I could do another live interview with BBC Radio Leicester. It went well but afterwards, as usual, I fretted that I might have given wrong impressions or failed to say something important. I was anxious that I didn't imply that I was enjoying a fabulous long holiday at other people's expense. Perhaps I worried too much about what other people thought.

We went to church with Jenny, Chas and Emily. It was a family service, with a congregation of only about thirty people. There were a handful of small children and some older boys and girls in scouts. Five or six scout leaders came. I saw two older ladies and another six or seven people. It felt very thin.

Jen led worship, played the piano, and acted out a drama sketch with Chas. She'd written a fabulous script, along the lines of Channel Four's *Grand Designs*, to demonstrate the building of the wall of Jerusalem by Nehemiah.

After a lovely roast dinner I packed and set off again. Leaving Jennifer was hard for us both but I know that our separation was much harder for her to bear, especially as she returned home without me. For me, the days were full of new things. I kept thinking how it would be lovely to share them with her. For Jennifer, the only thing different is my absence, and that's much tougher.

Separating from family and meeting again confirmed how much I loved them all and was proud of them.

I was asked during the radio interview about being on my own and during the day I thought about it further. As I said, I wasn't lonely, but I did feel the isolation. It made me think of people who have isolation forced upon them, by bereavement, divorce or redundancy. I counted my blessings and spent much of the day with my family in my thoughts.

I walked along broad tree-lined avenues and narrower streets of ex-council homes, through the Bournemouth suburbs of Moordown, into Ensbury Park and Northbourne. The map showed how surprisingly big the Poole-Bournemouth-Christchurch conurbation is and I reckoned I had walked fifteen miles through residential districts.

When I reached the River Stour things opened up and I picked up the Stour Valley Way footpath. The broad tracks reminded me of France's footpaths. The rain that had led me to put on my cumbersome waterproof over-trousers had long stopped, and it was a relief to cool down again without them. It was a gusty day, typical of early April and so a bit disappointing for the middle of May.

I paused to rest on a bench at the tenth tee of a golf-course and chatted with a couple of ladies who were waiting to play.

"Are you walking far?" they asked politely.

"Oh... about five hundred miles."

From the golf course the path led me onto the boundary of a beautifully-kept cricket pitch. Sadly, no match was in progress. The short springy grass was wonderful to walk on and I gave a moment's thought to the variety of surfaces that I'd encountered: pavements and roads, gravel tracks, rocky paths, hard-packed soil and grass of various lengths. I hadn't expected how significant, and how fascinating, this variety of textures would be.

I struggled at a kissing-gate, which wasn't designed for walkers with rucksacks. It took me three or four attempts to squeeze through. If Jennifer had been with me, I would have pecked her cheek as I did so.

Canford Magna is, without question, a pretty village. But I found it hard to like. Can a village look like it knows it's pretty? I think Canford Magna does, like a charmless girl who knows that she's attractive.

The village is dominated by Canford School, co-educational, full-boarding and independent. Access to its fabulous and rather beautiful facilities comes at the hefty price of £21,000 a year.

The huge and impressive main buildings of the school were designed by Charles Barry, for the iron magnate Ivor Guest, the first Baron Wimborne. Guest's family owned the largest ironworks in the world but he preferred Dorset's vales to the

Welsh valleys and the company of English aristocrats to his fellow countrymen. The magazine *Vanity Fair* mocked his snobbery and social climbing by referring to him as "the paying Guest."

Let me be honest and confess my distaste for the purchase of educational advantage. The uncharitable response to my Christian Aid collection in Bournemouth's comfortable suburbs was still infuriating me. Here among the properly wealthy I found myself further angered. I couldn't help thinking of the Welsh foundry workers, by whose poorly-rewarded sweat and skill this enormous mansion was built in the first place. Ivor Guest had succeeded to his father's private fortune and baronetcy, before being elevated to the peerage in the late nineteenth century. The Guest family sold the house to the school in the twentieth century and, while it is described as "unpretentious" by the *Good School Guide*, I find it hard to imagine too many descendants of the iron-workers boarding in the luxury acquired through their forefathers' labour.

In walking, I was seeing something of the extent of the inequalities in our land. Driving a car expands urban space by its relatively low speed, and compresses rural space into a fast blur. Walking plainly revealed the simple truth that ours is an enormous, spacious, un-cramped land. It's a popular myth that the land has been almost entirely built over, and that little open space is left. It suits those who own the land to promote the myth.

Walking allowed me to look into the front gardens of the suburbs, the balconies of cramped flats, and through wrought-iron gates into the vast properties of the wealthy. This became more apparent as my journey unfolded to me in the weeks to come. Short distances separated the places where the poor and the rich live. Hundreds of those who lived in the grimmest of Bournemouth's confined corners could have ample homes on one fairway of Canford School's private golf course, just four miles distant. The proximity is scandalous. The difference between these kinds of estate isn't apparent in the normal course of things, unless it's in front of your eyes, hour after hour, day after day.

The Stour Valley Way led me along the long drive to the old house, towards Wimborne. Along the way, it took me under one of the grandest and most ornate railway bridges I had ever seen. The railway line that it once carried is now gone and the drive that it spans is now a walker's path, rather than a splendid drive for the country house.

Perhaps it was my walking verse for the day that also agitated me to think of these things. It was from Isaiah 3.16 and 17 and the prophet announces divine judgement against those who set out their wealth to impress: *The Lord said, "Because the daughters of Zion are haughty and walk with outstretched necks, glancing wantonly with their eyes, mincing along as they go, tinkling with their feet; the Lord will afflict with scabs the heads of the daughters of Zion, and the Lord will lay bare their secret parts".*

The context for these prophetic words was the failure of a nation, not just the problem of louche girls. The graphic metaphor portrays the shaming of those who spend too long and too much on being admired, rather than living justly and generously. It follows God's exhortation in the previous verses that the nation should *cease to do evil, learn to do good; seek justice, rescue the oppressed, defend the orphan, plead for the widow.*

It made me think about the beautiful and prosperous England in which I would be walking during the coming week. By contrast, at the week's end I would be sleeping in one of the poorest communities in the land.

I crossed the Stour south of Wimborne, too late for evensong at the Minster, and climbed the hill to find Kinly Lodge, my resting place for the night.

Carolyn showed me around my two-storey accommodation, far more spacious than I needed, and I settled down with a sandwich of tasty roast beef from the dinner that Chas had cooked. Another nine miles walked, making two hundred and thirty four so far.

Wimborne Minster to Bristol - 98 miles across beautiful country

Chapter Six - Wimborne Minster to Bristol

I nipped into the Minster at Wimborne before I headed out of the town. Slowly walking through the north aisle I eavesdropped on a fascinating conversation about the structures of the Church of England, team ministries and the shaping new patterns of clergy deployment. A team from another diocese were visiting to make a documentary film to support their plans for following a "minster model" in response to falling clergy numbers. Most dioceses are grouping parishes together in some form of affiliation, as a way of managing reductions. The archdeacon in the group visiting the Minster told me, "nobody much likes it". By contrast, the minster model is about identifying strongest churches from which to base mission to a much wider area than a parish. Under this scheme other local churches would continue as part of a co-ordinated mission, rather than for their own sake alone.

The minster model proposes a more effective use of resources, a focus on mission and sustainability. But the chief difficulty in shifting the Church of England towards any modification of its historic parish system is its organic nature, its being a "located community", rather than a national franchise. At its best, this means that the Church can be wonderfully available.

The difficulty for archdeacons, or anyone else thinking creatively about reshaping churches for mission, is that this kind of organism usually defies organisation. Change can be invited, fostered, but rarely enforced. Even if it were possible to be systematic about mission and ministry in the Church of England, most people recognise that something precious would be lost. Various plausible models for change are advanced from time to time but while each contains real value, none provides a complete answer.

The Church of England runs a mixed economy; different strategies at the same time. At times it feels like a group of people playing *Monopoly*, chess, *Cluedo* and poker on the same table, all at the same time. As long as everyone keeps taking turns, rolling dice, moving pieces, shuffling, dealing and collecting £200 when they pass GO, looking all the time as though they know what they're doing, it's possible to believe there might even be an underlying strategy. If no one asks any questions, things simply keep going. But if they do, they're met with incomprehension by the other players: "Your question makes no sense in the game I'm playing!"

I followed the Stour Valley Way once again, and the quiet road which runs between high hedges up to Blandford Forum. Between the thatched houses and Dorset oaks, meadows of buttercups, cow parsley and long grasses were churned by a blustery wind. The breeze flung cloud shadows up the lane and everything was in motion. It was a beautiful early summer's day.

I spotted mayflies dancing in the air beneath the trees near the river. But no sign, at least to my eyes, of the dreaded Blandford Fly. This small black insect has a nasty, sometimes even fatal, bite. For the last twenty years the authorities have sprayed pesticide to reduce the numbers and cases have dropped dramatically as a result.

In Shapwick, I found a sign on the village green, which was recently dedicated in the name of Charles Bennett. He was born in the village and became Britain's first olympic gold medallist in a track and field event. Bennett won the 1500 metres race in Paris in 1900 in a record time of four minutes, six seconds.

Bennett would no doubt have raced up the same lane that I was walking for his training, perhaps up to Tarrant Crawford and back. Or up the hill to the ancient Badbury Rings.

Sticking to my rather slower pace, I walked on past enormous country estates and fields of cattle. Again I wondered who's England I was walking in.

Blandford has a good feel to it. The centre was completely destroyed by fire in the 1730's and rebuilt by the Bastard family in a consistent restrained Georgian style. I found a blue plaque on the wall of the King's Arms where I was staying. It recorded that the pub was built on the site of the tallow works where the fire started.

In the fish and chip shop I met Dale and James, two young soldiers from the signals regiment training at the nearby army camp. We talked as we waited for our chips to be fried.

I joined them on a bench outside the church. We chatted about the town, their forthcoming posting to Stafford, and my walk. Their army world is so all-involving and though they've been in Blandford for a year, it still feels to them as though they're just passing through the town. I thought more about the "church bubble" in which I spend my time and was thankful for the rare chance of our two worlds meeting.

"What about the chaplains?" I asked. "Do you see much of them?"

Ryan said that they did get to see them as part of the character-formation classes in their training. "The padre asks us what we think about things." he added.

James said, "They're always smiling! When you see the padre, he's always smiling."

In *The Dolphin*, I recognised Laurie's accent. He told me he was from Wolverhampton, and we connected places in our pasts. I normally sit at a table in a pub, but this time I stood at the bar and talked with Kieran, the other barman, and the regulars. It was a good way to find out more about the town. Kieran's keen to leave Blandford, having lived here all his life. But I heard from others that Dorset is "England's most beautiful county", that there's nowhere better.

During the day I had sat on a stile for lunch and to listen to the news. I had asked Jennifer to bring a radio down to Bournemouth. I didn't want it to change the silent nature of my walk but every few days on less interesting parts of the route, I listened in to the news. I learned that a row about MPs expenses was damaging the reputation of parliament

Appropriately for a day in which party politics was on my mind, my walking verse for the day was Isaiah 30.21 *"When you turn to the right or when you turn to the left, your ears shall hear a word behind you, saying, 'This is the way; walk in it.'"*

—

I began Day Twenty Seven with the worst breakfast of my entire walk. At *The King's Arms* I was served cold beans, overcooked bacon and wrinkled sausages that contained a strange-tasting dark meat that I couldn't identify. I should have guessed that things weren't going to be good when after accepting the offer of a cooked breakfast it was served to me within five minutes. I reckon most of the ingredients had been pre-cooked, goodness knows how many days before.

On the way out of Blandford Forum I rang ahead to the bed

and breakfast in Stalbridge that I had booked. This was something I did each day. When I had made the reservations, I noted how varied the response of the landlords and landladies was. Some asked for deposits, some sent out letters of confirmation and some asked me to call them before I arrived, "just in case we forget". I thought it prudent to call ahead each morning, just in case there was a misunderstanding. On Day Twenty Seven, there was.

"Hi," I said, "I'm booked in to stay with you tonight, and I just thought I would ring ahead to confirm what time I'll be with you."

"Tonight?" The lady said.

"That's right. My name is Simon Harvey. I'm booked in for one night."

"Er..." the hesitation worried me. "We don't do accommodation any more. We gave it up at Easter."

The lady was sure that she hadn't accepted a booking from me, so it looked as if I had slipped up. This was the first time that I had had a problem with my reservations and my heart sank. I knew Stalbridge was a small place which was unlikely to have anywhere else to stay.

"Do you know of any other accommodation in Stalbridge?" I asked hopefully.

"No."

"Okay, thanks."

Under a heavy cloud and increasing drizzle, I quickly thought through my options.

I could walk a double distance either on this day or the next, to reach Sparkford, my destination for the end of Day Twenty Eight. But that would be twenty-seven miles and it was already after eleven o'clock. I didn't fancy returning to the grotty King's Arms for another night either.

The second option was to get a taxi or find a bus to reach Sparkford. This was the easiest way to get back on track but it would mean giving up the plan to walk every step of the way. How would I feel, I wondered, to explain to everyone that I had walked all but twenty seven miles of the journey? Taking transport would also speed me to my destination in less than an hour, leaving me a lot of time to rue my mistake, making for a miserable day.

The third option was to find an alternative to the failed booking in Stalbridge.

Worried that something in my planning had gone seriously wrong and that the itinerary was beginning to unravel, I rang *The Sparkford Inn* where I was due to stay in two days' time. It was a relief to hear that they had me booked in on the correct night. I asked the man at *The Sparkford Inn* for recommendations for somewhere en route. He suggested *The Half Moon Inn* in Sherborne.

Sherborne was a good deal farther than Stalbridge. The day's walk was already planned at thirteen miles and a quick look at the map showed that a new route to Sherborne would be at least twenty. I was also approaching the hills of north Dorset and it was clear that I would need to do make some ascents as well. It was going to be a long, slow day.

Nevertheless, I rang the *Half Moon* and made a reservation. Praying for endurance, I set off across the River Stour and out into the hills. I had already picked up a Cornish pasty from the local bakery and I worked out a way of rationing it over the next ten hours, on the assumption that my new rural route probably wouldn't include a shop.

The rain showers quickly disappeared and over the first hour I took off layers, so that I spent almost all of the blustery day in a tee shirt, which was just about warm enough when I was moving.

The new route included unplanned treasures. The gradual climb to Bulbarrow Hill was rewarded with views as beautiful as any I've seen so far. Rawlsbury Camp is an Iron Age hill fort, in a remarkable spot, overlooking a broad valley to the east and the rippled landscape of small fields, the winding river and woods to the west and north. This lovely geology was part of the same Upper Cretaceous chalk as the French Pays de Caux, through which I had walked two weeks before.

I met a couple of men who were putting up signs for the following weekend's *Cycle Challenge* - three hundred and fifty miles in three days. That sounded tough to me, especially as we were talking while they fixed their sign to another indicating a 1-in-5 gradient. They asked about my walking and were amazed at what I was doing.

"You look like you're still in good shape!" said one.

I said I wasn't sure about that. But thinking about it later on, it was true that I seemed to be coping with the physical ordeal of walking and I gave thanks to God while praying for strength and stamina to survive this longest of days.

The lanes led me through a succession of small villages with wonderful names: Stoke Wake, Wonston, Hazlebury Bryan, Droop, King's Stag, Bishop's Caundle and Alweston.

In Hazlebury Bryan, the pub was shut. But a collection of signs pointed to the general store on the village green. Not much bigger than a garden shed (and looking just like one with its lapped timber and roof-felt) the little shop creaked in the strong wind that blew across the cricket pitch. It served as a Post Office on Mondays, and sold a remarkably wide range of goods. I bought a cold drink from the fridge, an apple and and a banana but I could have also had a hot pie, an ice cream or a bag of potatoes.

"Was it clear on Bulbarrow Hill?" asked the shopkeeper.

"Yes, I could see all the way to the horizon. It was lovely."

"Shit!"

I was surprised, not only by his expletive but at his sorrow that I should have enjoyed good weather on the hill.

"That means rain then," he continued. "If it's clear on Bulbarrow Hill, it's sure to rain."

I wondered what patterns of terrain and winds would lead to this mysterious combination of clear skies and rain but was too tired to debate his meteorology.

The hours passed slowly from this point. I tried not to think about the distance but instead about time. I knew that at the pace I was making, it would be at least seven thirty by the time I made it to Sherborne. So rather than measure my progress against a predicted schedule (which I knew would be depressing) I resolved to simply keep walking into the evening.

By now I was going terribly slowly, just over two miles an hour, including rest stops. These pauses were vital however; I had made the mistake before of not resting and suffered the exhausting consequences.

At the end of a long day's walking I had moved on a kind of autopilot. It was easy just to keep going and not to rest at all but the result is always a deeper exhaustion and strained muscles. So I forced myself to take a five or ten minute break on the hour, every hour. These were proper breaks: rucksack off, sitting down (sometimes on a convenient bench, sometimes perched in the verge of the road), stretching and giving my aching leg muscles a massage. I also took a standing rest on the half-hour for a few moments.

The hours passed and the sun fell beneath the tops of the hedges. I was on the A-road now so flew my bright orange pennant from my waistband. Thankfully tractors and lorries were infrequent but when they passed I pressed myself into the hedge, sideways on to the road.

By now I had enough experience of road walking to notice that lorry and tractor drivers are actually very good. They anticipated their braking and steering a long way in advance. Older drivers pottering along were also very generous, pulling out wide to give me space. Perhaps surprisingly, the youngest drivers were also very good, even if they travelled a bit fast. The problem group was my own - the middle-aged. I noticed how distracted or unobservant they were. They swerved at the last minute and seemed to think that I only need inches of clearance. It's funny how consistent this pattern was, on both French and English roads.

Eventually, at ten past eight, I arrived at *The Half Moon* Inn. Too tired to eat, I carried a pint of *Abbot Ale* to my room, filled a deep, hot bath and then slept for nine hours.

My walking verse for the day was Isaiah 59.9: *Justice is far from us, and righteousness does not reach us; we wait for light, and lo! there is darkness; and for brightness, but we walk in gloom.*

The verse offers a different experience from my Day Twenty Seven. I had walked over twenty-one miles, farther than I had ever walked in a day. I prayed with thanksgiving for the fact that I had been given the strength to make it. I hadn't, after all, walked in gloom.

–

One of the best ways to enjoy an ancient building is to put yourself within overhearing distance of a tour guide. The best guides know when to speak and when to stop. Most ramble on for too long. It's much better to be an eavesdropper, drifting in and out at will.

I was in just this position on the morning of Day Twenty

Eight, as I sat writing postcards in the nave of Sherborne Abbey. The guide shepherded his little flock of tourists to the top of the nave and once assembled, cleared his throat, and began.

"Welcome to Sherborne Abbey. Although we've just celebrated our thirteen hundredth anniversary, we're not a museum. We're a living church."'

My ears pricked up. He went on to talk very briefly about the way the church community seeks to serve the people of Sherborne today, before beginning the historical story. It was gently done, and this little huddle of tourists were clearly informed that the story of Christian faith in Sherborne is still being written.

The first thing to notice about the Abbey is the gorgeous stone of which it is built. Simon Jenkins reckons the ham stone is "the loveliest building material in England". I first thought that the best way to describe it was 'honey-coloured', but honey isn't a rich enough shade. It later occurred to me that it's precisely the colour of bruised root ginger.

After musing about the disconnection between church and general population which I've noticed as I walk, it was fascinating to hear about the most dramatic moment in the abbey's history.

The building had served as the seat of bishops in the kingdom of Wessex from 705 to 1075. When the bishops moved out to Old Sarum, a community of Benedictine monks moved in.

A separate church for the people of the parish was built next door, but it wasn't fully consecrated. So for baptisms and funerals the population had to come into the Abbey, whose monks, it seems, weren't at all interested in them. The Abbey community were inwardly-focussed, oblivious to the needs of the ordinary people of the town.

By the fifteenth century this tension had deepened. A mob

descended on the Abbey to protest about its inaccessibility and broke in. During the commotion one hot-head let loose a flaming arrow, which lodged high up in a carved wooden screen. The flames soon spread upwards, into the roof and melted the lead. The blaze engulfed the whole building.

I thought of today's walking verse, Isaiah 65.2: *I held out my hands all day long to a rebellious people, who walk in a way that is not good, following their own devices.*

Was it Sherborne's angry mob who had rebelled against God? Or was it the monastic community, inward-looking and uninterested in the people, who had forgotten to be outreaching?

The abbey's present harmonious style, with its sumptuous fan-vaulting and elaborate ceiling bosses, owes its origins to the scale of the rebuilding project. I liked it so much I thought it should enter the short-list of my favourite church buildings.

I headed out of the one-time capital of Wessex along *The Macmillan Way,* named for the Macmillan Cancer Relief charity. I bumped into Nick and Pauline, a couple of walkers who were studying their map.

"We're from Berkshire. Near Broadmoor Hospital!"

We got talking and shared the road for a mile or two.

Nick's brother was just about to complete the pilgrimage route to Santiago de Compostella. During my walk, I've heard of several people doing this but none as old as Nick's brother, who is seventy!

Nick joins his brother in Western Australia each year to tackle another section of a long-distance route, the *Bibbulmun Track* from Perth to Albany. It sounded like a different kind of walking experience from mine, with rudimentary huts every ten to twenty miles along the trail instead of bed and breakfast accommodation. Nick and his brother fill their flasks with rainwater and take enough provisions for the four or five days distance between towns. That's *real* adventure.

I enjoyed sharing the path with other people for the first time in my twenty-eight days.

I shared another short section of the journey with two horse riders. I let them pass and followed them down the narrow lane. Horses, I noticed, walk quite clumsily. Watching the way their wonky hind legs vault along, ending each stride with a flick of a hoof, I thought that walking is the horse's least elegant way of locomotion. There's no grace in a walking horse's bottom.

I paused at *The Mitre* in Sandford Orcas and settled down with a pint of *Reverend Awdry* ale. I think that the author of the *Thomas the Tank Engine* books had Gloucestershire connections, but perhaps the landlord of the *Mitre* is following the ecclesiastical theme of his pub with his choice of beers.

Blessed by the good Reverend, I set off again by way of Staffords Green, Corton Denham, Girt, Sutton Montis and into Sparkford.

The church of Mary Magdalene at Sparkford was open. It was a neat and tidy kind of place, clearly well used for worship. I liked the fifties stylised statuette of the deposition by William Thornton, and the 1977 painting of the cross by a certain A. Heinke near the door.

Sparkford is unlike any of the other villages I had passed that day, developed into a ribbon of houses, workshops and factories. The railway line accounted for its size and industry and still passes through but without a station to stop at.

Opposite *The Sparkford Inn*, where I was staying, is the headquarters of The Haynes Group, best known for their fabulously meticulous *Owners Workshop Manuals* for almost every model of car sold in the United Kingdom since the nineteen sixties.

I own several, and in the days when I tackled my own car maintenance, the grubbiest of their grease-thumbed pages revealed which parts of my particular car gave me most trouble.

The Haynes buildings had a lovely "British engineering" feel about them. The steel concertina door leading from the road was marked, *Haynes Project Research Workshop* and beyond it lay, I imagined, bearded, pipe-smoking, head-scratching gents dismantling vehicles. Behind doors such as these, I mused, we British used to build jet engines, rockets and hovercraft.

I wondered what business is like for Haynes these days. Modern cars offer little scope for tinkering for the owner. Manufacturers guard their secrets carefully, making it hard for independent garages to service their cars without special tools and diagnostic equipment.

Thankfully by now all that was left of the injury to my right leg was a slight swelling on my shin. But during the walk I had been collecting various minor ailments and tribulations. I thought it was about time I offered readers of my daily blog a summary of them, with names of my own devising:

Squelchy foot - This appeared on the way to Wimborne after walking on stony paths. I first noticed an odd clicking sensation on the outer part of the sole of my right foot. The funny feeling grew during the week and 'squelchy' is the best description I could find for it. It wasn't painful exactly, feeling as though the tissues and ligaments had become mushy, as my feet were more flat-footed than ever.

Nettle elbow - caused by brushing the hedgerows as I walk. Various lumps, bumps, prickles and spots.

Blacktoe - a curious blackened nail on the big toe of my right foot, of uncertain provenance.

Strappitch - just what it says.

Pocket blisters - on the tips of my fingers, caused by the constant flicking of my trouser pockets as I walk.

Stile victim - one who has stumbled at the crossing into a field.

Stile guru - one who has mastered the art.

In addition, I had one or two issues of a digestive nature, the effect on my intestines of daily doses of real ale and walking being somewhat fermentational!

Day Twenty Nine was very close to a perfect walking day.

Slipping out of Sparkford and almost immediately into Somerset, I found my way through lanes heavy with hawthorn blossom and the scent of wild garlic.

Cumulus clouds were building through the morning and their dark grey bases looked like they were keen to dispense rain.

But there were plenty of gaps and in a gentle breeze the day felt positively summer-y. The shaded parts of the lane were cool and it was never too hot to be comfortable.

The Harriers and helicopters of RNAS Yeovilton were up and about. I found my way under their hovering through South Barrow to Babcary.

My walking verse for the day was one of my favourites of the whole route. My friend Colin had also spotted it and included it in a card he sent before I set off. It was Jeremiah 6.16: *Stand at the crossroads, and look, and ask for the ancient paths, where the good way lies; and walk in it, and find rest for your souls.*

It was providential that this should be my verse on a day when I crossed the Fosse Way, the ancient Roman road which would have taken me directly to Leicester if I had stayed on it. I managed to walk it for only a mile and I reckon it would have led me to an early grave rather than Leicester. It was viciously fast, with tiny verges and huge lorries.

I got to the crossroads at Lydford-on-Fosse and thought of the verse. This spot surely is a crossroads at one of Britain's ancient paths if ever there was one.

Workmen were rebuilding the front of a house at the junction and I made some remark about the danger of the road. One of them told me that the house they were working on was partially demolished by a Land Rover which two years previously had hurtled through the junction and clipped another car. The Landrover ended up in the front lounge and its driver was found asleep in the foot well.

I looked again at the half-destroyed house and wondered about the family who'd been living behind temporary shuttering while the insurance was sorted out. The junction was a frightful place and I couldn't imagine living there.

I had stood at this crossroads and looked, and asked. Though this ancient path is still very much used, there was scarcely any sign of rest for souls. The real "way" of peace is not a physical way, or a mappable route. The Way of Life, the Gospel of John records, is not a track or highway, he's a person, Jesus Christ.

On to Keinton Mandeville, where I lunched at *The Quarry Inn*. The place looked like a really well-run pub, and there were plenty of patrons as I enjoyed a huge jacket potato and pint of well-kept *Exmoor Ale*. After lunch I descended from Barton St David through Butleigh to the levels and the skies cleared. I glimpsed Glastonbury Tor through the trees and wondered how many thousands of pilgrims had fixed their eyes on it during the last part of their journey to the Abbey.

Somerset's cows seemed more curious than Dorset's. Every time I passed a field, they wandered across to check me out.

I arrived at *The Abbey House*, the retreat centre for the Diocese of Bath and Wells. I wanted to return there as soon as I planned my walk. My only previous visit was for the three-day selection panel which led to me being recommended for ordination training.

It was over a decade since my visit but stepping into the various rooms I found to my amazement that I could recall the conversations that took place. The power of associative memory is remarkable. The largest room was where we were first briefed and where we sat a strange multiple-choice intelligence test. This involved matching a lot of shapes in an exercise that might be useful in ministry only if I am ever required to repair a stained glass window. In another room I remembered a casual conversation with exhausted fellow candidates awaiting one-to-one interviews. I sat and typed notes in one of the interview rooms where I answered pastoral ministry questions.

In the large drawing room we underwent one of the strangest experiences of the selection conference. We sat as a group of about eight, around a table on which there were sheets of typed paper.

These gave us brief notes about a fictional parish which we were going to discuss, under the scrutiny of the selectors, who sat with writing pads in their laps around the edge of the room. Our pieces of paper were all different, each describing a particular issue affecting the parish in question. We had ten minutes each in which to outline the issue and chair a discussion.

It was a gruelling experience. The young man who went first set about explaining his particular topic. The more he talked, the more nervous he got. I could see that in between his increasingly confused sentences he was taking shorter and shorter snatches of breath.

The tension built and we all became nervous for him. It would have been kind to interject with a comment but he scarcely left time between his frantic explanations. Eventually, as we shot each other anxious glances, he burst into the face of the woman who was sitting next to him, "So what do you think?"

She squealed. The selectors all inhaled deeply and started scribbling. We knew he had blown it.

Revisiting the Abbey House reminded me how very small I felt in the processes of the Church of England. Now, as Warden of Readers, I'm responsible organising the selection of candidates for ministry in our diocese and, for their sakes, I never want to forget how nerve-wracking the whole experience can be.

I popped into Glastonbury town centre to buy a sandwich for dinner. The town has as many loopy shops selling spells, crystals, and mystic nonsense as it always has. The characters on the street look much as they did all those years ago and the smells of patchouli and cannabis still drift up the main street.

This must be the fourth or fifth time I've visited and, oddly enough, the second time on a pilgrimage of sorts. The previous occasion was a rather bizarre day in which I accompanied parishioners and clergy from my placement church in Bristol to the annual Glastonbury Pilgrimage for catholic parishes in the Church of England. I had tried to lay aside my evangelical reservations and smiled at the thurifers' competitive incense-swinging in procession along the main street. The service in the grounds of the Abbey was only tolerable.

This time I sat on a bench eating a sandwich and banana dinner, accompanied by a homeless man with a dog on a piece of string. I then joined the congregation at St John the Baptist for an Ascension Day service of Holy Communion.

—

Sister Annverena, a member of the *Companions of Jesus the Good Shepherd* in Oxfordshire, joined me for breakfast at Glastonbury's Abbey House. We compared stories of walking alone through France, she having walked from Dieppe to Paris many years before.

We were soon joined by Janet and Ann, members of the Diocese of Exeter's Mothers' Union, whose annual retreat was concluding. It was a jolly breakfast, no fry-up but lots of toast, *Weetabix* and lovely prunes.

I tried typing notes on my Bluetooth keyboard, which had been failing in the previous days. It was a fantastic accessory, allowing me to type on a full-size keyboard and sending the keystrokes to my fancy mobile phone. It never did look very durable though and bit by plasticky bit, it fell apart. I had to resort to tapping away at the phone's screen with a tiny stylus and ended up pecking out more than ten thousand words for the blog like this.

Glastonbury has one of my favourite public signs. Carved

into the wall next to a drinking fountain by the Methodist Church is this gem: *PUBLIC NOTICE - COMMIT NO NUISANCE.*

It's so gloriously vague I reckon the chosen wording was the culmination of interminable committee meetings. I imagined a group of councillors negotiating a compilation of their pet topics until, well after midnight, someone who was keen to get home found a form of words that encompassed the prohibition of every possible civic misdemeanour. I wonder what, if any, effect on public order resulted from its injunction.

Another gem of a sign came to me at the Glastonbury Pilgrim Centre: *WE HAVE MOVED.* It would have been nice to find out what happens in the centre but alas, it had moved off my route.

I didn't feel much solidarity with the pilgrims to Glastonbury. The town is cursed with more than its fair share of bonkers Christian mythology to go along with all the other hocus pocus. For example, the reddish waters of the *Chalice Well* are caused by a significant amount of iron oxide in the water. Legend tells that Joseph of Arimathea, who lent his grave for the burial of Jesus Christ, collected drops of his blood in a chalice, which he buried in the very same well.

This kind of nonsense shouldn't, of course, get past a first telling without someone raising a hand with, "Hang on a minute..."

I felt I could hardly blame the pagans for their wacky shops when this sort of thing had been fostered in my own faith tradition.

The lanes north of Glastonbury are untidy and unattractive. A notice outside what looked like a scrapyard advertised CABBAGE PLANTS 3P EACH. When did I last see anything for threepence, I wondered. I looked around and seeing no fields of cabbages, I began to wonder if this was some euphemistic advertisement for some other kind of popular and unlawful local shrub.

Compared with the cosy vales of Dorset and the South Somerset hills, the moors of drained peat marsh were rather *plain*. I crossed East Backwear, was surprised that a settlement as small as Godney has its own church. Godney also boasts a surprising number of pill boxes, from which machine guns could be aimed across the watery levels. This was because it formed a vital link in the GHQ Line during the Second World War. The General Headquarters Line was a series of fortifications and defences that were designed to halt the feared German invasion of England. At least, it was hoped, it might tie up the advancing Nazi hoard for a day or two. At Godney, the bridges across the ditches and rivers that drained the levels were mined, so that with a few detonations, the advancing Panzers would be stopped in (or off) their tracks.

Where Hitler's divisions might have stumbled, I pressed north, taking to the hills again at Bleadney.

I was ready for a good lunch and at *The Panborough Inn* I got one. Two courses, of whitebait and vegetable lasagne, accompanied by *Cheddar Ales' Gorge Best*.

The road took me through Theale and Latcham to Wedmore, whose road-signs proclaim its significance as the place where King Arthur made peace. On looking further into it, I discovered that Arthur had first defeated his Viking enemies in battle, then rather than executing them, invited them to consider being baptised as Christians. The Vikings were not in the mind to be martyred, so agreed to the sacrament. To mark their incorporation into the body of Christian believers, Arthur threw a big party for them, which he held in Wedmore. It's mission of a sort, I supposed.

The walking verse for the day was Jeremiah 6.25: *Do not go out into the field, or walk on the road, for the enemy has a sword, terror is on every side.*

I was glad things had calmed down since the battles of

Arthur and the preparations for an invasion in 1940. I thought of the Danes in their defeat, going to sleep that night in Wedmore with full stomachs, music in their ears and a new faith.

Down through Cocklake and Clewer and I moved onto Cheddar Moor. Grass for silage was being collected on the lower slopes of the hills and I stopped to watch the skill of the drivers. One vehicle whirled its spinning rakes to scoop up the grass and blew it from a spout into a trailer towed by another tractor. It was fascinating teamwork.

I reached my bed and breakfast on the outskirts of Cheddar not long after five o'clock. I noticed that I had now walked over three hundred miles.

–

Simon and Lisa gave me the kind of hearty breakfast I was hoping for with such a big challenge ahead of me. Day Thirty One was always going to be a tough one, with two big climbs and over eighteen miles to Bristol.

I had jotted down my walking verse for the day from Jeremiah 10.23: *I know, O Lord, that the way of human beings is not in their control, that mortals as they walk cannot direct their steps.*

I wasn't sure that I agreed with Jeremiah. After all, I had been reading lots of verses in which God invited human beings to make good choices about how they walked in life. The rest of the book challenges Jeremiah's claim by announcing that his countrymen have brought calamity on themselves precisely because of their waywardness.

Cheddar was already busy with tourists on the Saturday of a sunny Bank Holiday. In addition to the usual crowds, the roads were also full of cyclists, hundreds of them panting up the gorge in a glowing bright procession of sweaty Lycra.

I followed the road at a less breathless pace past the caves and souvenir shops. I spotted the one that had fuelled a merry afternoon's climb with a gallon of rough cider when I came here with friends on holiday as a nineteen year old. I decided it would be unwise to repeat the experience this time.

The Gorge is one of England's natural wonders and still impresses after a number of visits. It narrows as the road climbs and the cliffs become steeper. In addition to the cyclists there were plenty of walkers and climbers about, and a convoy of vintage Jaguar cars came down the hill.

I left the road through a gate and headed up *Velvet Bottom*, a path that lead past the Black Rock and the valley where lead ore was mined and refined. The Romans exploited the mineral deposits, which continued to be worked right up to the nineteenth century. Sure enough, the grass was as velvety as the name promised, and was cropped like snooker baize by the huge colonies of rabbits.

By now it was becoming a gloriously sunny day. The high clouds thinned and the sun grew hotter by the minute.

I had climbed to eight hundred and fifty feet and the going was on the slow side of steady. Sadly, when I reached the *Wellsway Inn* it was closed. I checked *Google Maps* on my phone and it confirmed that the next pub on the route was *The Blue Bowl*. I rang ahead to make sure they were open.

After lunch I walked along the west shore of Chew Valley Lake and up into Chew Stoke. One fork in the road offered me a Bunyan-esque choice between Pilgrim Road and Pagan's Hill. King Arthur's Viking foes might have worried about the decision, I had no qualms nor superstitions. The former would have taken me well off my route, so I plumped for the latter. I didn't spot any pagans but then, how would I have known?

Up Chew Hill and then even steeper climbs to Maiden Head

at the top of Dundry Hill. The heat had intensified but there was no haze to dull the spectacular panorama. The Welsh hills lay clearly beyond the two Severn suspension bridges and Bristol directly before me. I knew the city well enough to pick out a dozen landmarks.

The road led down to Withywood, where crowds of drinkers stood in the sunshine outside the pubs. Bored toddlers milled between the pushchairs while parents supped pints of *Carling* lager from glasses held by flabby hands. The first hot week of the spring had led to some unwise clothing choices - sunburnt flesh spilling over taught fabric that during another, long ago summer, might have fitted. The mood of the gathering seemed to be teetering in that moment when good natured revelling slides into lairy aggression.

Into Bishopsworth and then eastwards to Hartcliffe. Hartcliffe is a strange nineteen fifties "outer estate", practically in the countryside but very disadvantaged and scoring badly on the government's "multiple indices of deprivation". For the first two decades of its existence many jobs were available at the enormous Imperial Tobacco factory. It has long since closed.

I walked up through the Novers Park Estate and into Knowle West. By now I was exhausted as well as hot. A group of young men lay on the green open space that I skirted. They shouted out to their friend, "Kieran!"

Kieran responded with a song, bellowed back at the top of his voice, "Let's get f-----g hammered! Nah, nah, nah, nah!"

And with that he danced past me into *Costcutter*, whose shelves were piled high with the super-strength brews that were obviously favoured by Kieran and friends. The Viking warrior friends of King Arthur might well have stocked up there if they had the chance.

Farther along the road I finally found St Barnabas Vicarage, the home of my friends, Alister and Sally.

–

We first met way back at the start of 1986. Jennifer and I were engaged to be married and had decided that in the New Year of 1986, we would book the date and venue for our wedding. I knew that Jennifer would want a church wedding - as a teenager she'd been actively involved with Holy Trinity Church in Heath Town, Wolverhampton, and she still had friends there. It left me, though, with something of a problem.

At that time, at the age of twenty two, I had not a shred of Christian faith. I was certain in my belief that God was an invention of the human imagination, a projection of inner hopes and fears that allowed people to cope with the randomness of life by giving the appearance of meaning and purpose. Good friends had tried to persuade me that I should join them in believing but their arguments were unconvincing.

Worse, what I had encountered in the Church suggested hypocrisy and irrelevance. It appeared more interested in its own institution and playing peculiar games in even more peculiar clothing on Sunday mornings. It even involved *public singing*, something that I felt belonged only to the terraces at the Molineux where even I belted out songs in the cause of Wolverhampton Wanderers.

How could I stand in a church and make marriage vows in explicitly religious language, vows which implied that I believed in a God, when plainly I didn't?

But how could I disappoint Jennifer?

At the age of about seven, I remember clearly being asked in the school playground about my religious background.

"What religion are you?" a friend asked.

"Erm... I don't."

My friend laughed. "Yeah, yer do! Everyone has a religion: Church of England, Catholic, Methodist"

It didn't occur to him that the little list of options he gave me were all slightly different manifestations of the same Christian religion. I still looked blank.

"Okay," he continued. "When you was christened, where was it? Which church?"

Now I was on more certain ground. "I've never been christened. Our family doesn't believe in it."

"Yower kiddin'?" And with that he rounded up half a class of boys who circled me with real curiosity as though they'd discovered a new species.

"So, you ay a Christian?" one asked.

"No."

"Yo've never bin christened?" asked another.

"No."

"Everyone's bin christened!" announced someone else.

The little crowd muttered among themselves before melting away. Had I got this wrong? Were my parents pretending that I had not been christened? Why, what secret were they hiding? No, I was sure I was remembering correctly - my mum and dad complained every time religion appeared on the television. We never watched *Songs of Praise*. For the first time in my life, I felt uniquely irreligious.

The next day at school I regarded my classmates from the edge of the crowd, as one who didn't quite belong. They all knew what they were - mostly "C of E", but with a number of "Catholics" and a handful of Methodists.

Then at playtime, the friend who'd first raised the subject

came across to me, beaming a huge smile.

"I know what you are," he said. "I asked me dad. He says your a *heathen!*"

A heathen? I had never heard the word. "Heathen" - it didn't sound so bad.

"A heathen is someone who doh believe in God." explained my theologically informed mate. "Heathens doh go to church. Heathens doh get christened. That's what yo am - a *heathen!*"

He announced my newly defined status with glee to his friends who, having found a category for me, welcomed me back to the group. I quite enjoyed the status.

Fifteen years later, I resolved that for Jennifer's sake, I would be prepared to marry in church. After all, making the vows to Jennifer was the important part - what would it matter if these were wrapped in language about a fictional God? He didn't exist, and neither did any other spiritual power. I could demonstrate the meaninglessness of the religious mumbo jumbo precisely by being unafraid to use it.

I did reckon though, that there was a significant chance that the Church would decide that it wouldn't *want me.* I wouldn't have blamed them either. If asked about my religious beliefs I would be honest, nor would I conceal that I had not been baptised.

Sue, a Christian friend, told us that a new vicar had moved to the church at Heath Town. "He's really nice. His name is Alister, you'll get on with him very well." She added, "Oh, and he'll marry anybody!"

I told Jennifer that I really wanted her to have the church wedding that she hoped for, but that she should be prepared for being turned down on the grounds of my unbelief. To increase our chances of a welcome, I said that I was even prepared to go to church one Sunday and to approach the vicar after the service. (I thought this would be more likely to impress than simply phoning up with a request.)

One Sunday morning at the end of January 1986, we set off together for Holy Trinity Church. The huge black wooden door looked as though it were purposely designed to be off-putting. I paused and drew a deep breath. Come on, Simon, I thought. How bad could it be? Deciding that I could cope with an hour and a half of anything short of moderate physical violence, I tucked myself behind Jennifer and we went in.

To my astonishment, we were welcomed. Bill, one of the leaders of a children's group to which Jennifer had belonged, smiled and hugged her. He looked me in my eye and shook my hand. "Hello! Welcome!"

Much of the service that followed was the meaningless mumbo jumbo that I had expected. In those days the main service used the *Book of Common Prayer*, whose sixteenth century phrases seemed to have been designed to be as impenetrable as the black door had appeared. The hymns were unknown to me and similarly meaningless.

Half way through the service, the vicar stood in the pulpit to preach. I can't remember the Bible passages that Alister preached about, nor anything that he said. But I did remember the shocking relevance of it. During the sermon he spoke about the world that I recognised, about the social issues which had spurred me to be involved in local politics (before I left it again, disenchanted). He engaged me, addressed me as an adult, didn't try to simplify his faith into a condescending cartoon caricature but hinted at mystery, seriousness, profundity.

After the service we chose our moment. "We'd like to talk to you about getting married here." Jennifer asked nervously.

"Of course," smiled Alister. "Come and see me."

Church had not been what I thought it was going to be. The genuine welcome had been refreshing, I felt that people were sincerely interested in me. I had heard a lot about religion before. But I was sure I had never heard the gospel, in the way that Alister described it.

The next Sunday I went back, keen to hear more. I decided that the music and liturgy were hopeless and that rather than struggle to understand them I should simply ignore them. But Alister's sermons, they were worth hearing.

Within a fortnight, Alister and Sally had invited us to a meal. And now, twenty two years later, I was eating at their home again, talking late into the evening about all sorts of things - catching up on family news, shared friends and the challenges of being truly missional churches. There's more to tell about my conversion to Christianity but I'll save that for when my journey led me to Holy Trinity Church.

Alister had lost none of his radicalism nor his Tasmanian accent. Our conversation was as inspiring and stretching as usual. He approaches issues from outside the perspective of institutions; standing instead in solidarity with the poorest and excluded. In Knowle West he has shaped creative relational ministries, enabling the whole church in its engagement with the neighbourhood, rather than forming a dependent community around himself.

We talked a lot about sustainability, both in the context of changing patterns of ministry in the Church and the "low-energy future" that he foresees as impacting on society as a whole.

The Book of Lamentations supplied me a rather gloomy verse for the day. Verse eighteen of chapter four has this: *Our pursuers dogged our steps so that we could not walk in our streets.*

In the service at St Barnabas' Church, Alister interviewed me about my "backwards pilgrimage" and I was pleased to be able to tell his church how instrumental Sally and he had been in my coming to faith.

Sally cooked wonderful meals for us and we walked together through Blaise Castle and along Bristol Harbour. It was great to share this time with them.

Bristol to Tewkesbury - 74 miles along trading routes ancient and modern

Chapter Seven - Bristol to Tewkesbury

Having rested with Alister and Sally, for Day Thirty Three I had a short walk through Bristol, revisiting places that had become well known to me more than a decade before.

Knowle West is rather different from Knowle. Broad Walk led me up past the cricket pitch, into Knowle's more settled, less troubled streets. I turned north and walked along to the Church of Holy Nativity, where I had spent a bizarre but enjoyable six-weeks of Anglo-Catholicism during a college placement.

There is really only one Christian Church. All Christians who hold the basic truths of the faith belong together in one worldwide Church. My childhood friends were confused when they spoke of "Church of England", "Catholic" and "Methodist" as different religions. There is an essential unity in the global Church, which is truly wonderful. At times, it's possible to see the realisation of the Bible's promise, that *there is no longer Jew or Greek, slave or free, male and female; for we are all one in Christ Jesus.* But of course, the foibles of humanity meant that it didn't take long for factions and rivalries to split the early Church. We have ended up with a number of churches, which all hold to the basic unity of the one worldwide Church but who each do things slightly differently.

The Church of England, Methodist, Roman Catholic, Baptist and other churches have different systems of administration and governance. They also worship differently. Sometimes this comes as a result of thought-through theological principle and sometimes as a result of tradition. Sometimes tradition and theology are blended in a complicated mix that is difficult to untangle. You might think that the basic style of worship and life inside the Church of England would be pretty much the same wherever you went. It's not that simple.

One of the glories of the Church of England is the diversity of expression and emphasis of the same Christian faith. Some of its members prize the heritage of the pre-Reformation Catholic Church and their services are full of candles, incense, statues of Mary and other paraphernalia. At the other end of the spectrum, some conservative evangelicals dismiss virtually everything that doesn't appear in the description of the New Testament church.

Liberals and charismatics, open evangelicals, and Anglo-Catholics, or "middle of the road" - there's a wide variety of churches even within the Church of England. Some people choose to belong to a particular church because it consciously expresses one of these traditions. Most find themselves in a church through convenience, habit, or because they have found *the real thing* - the gospel outworked and embodied in a specific community. Frustratingly for the zealots, it appears possible for each tradition to be a vehicle for God's grace. Of course, most congregations include people from more than one of these traditions and many, if not most, people from no particular tradition at all.

Now, I'm an evangelical. Not, I hope, the kind of ranting hell-fire-and-brimstone stereotypes that are sometimes portrayed.

I'm an evangelical because at their best, evangelical churches emphasise the grace of God. Evangelicals tend to be ethusiastic about outward-looking mission, serving the wider community and making God known through the teaching and preaching of the Bible. Evangelicalism fits best my understanding of how the Church can be shaped for following, worshipping and serving God. But I recognise (and this is really important) that evangelicals do not have a monopoly on these things. Nor do we have nothing to learn from others. Nor do we have to make the conversion of other Christians to our way of doing things a greater priority than engaging with the world outside the church.

I became a Christian in an evangelical church and studied at an evangelical theological training college. While studying, the opportunity for a six-week parish placement arose and I was keen to explore something different. I had never experienced the Anglo-Catholic tradition of the Church of England and I was interested to see what it was all about.

"Please find me the church farthest from my own tradition." I asked the pastoral department who co-ordinated the church placements.

I ended up at Holy Trinity, Knowle, where each day began with a daily office (a short prayer service) strictly following the liturgy of the Roman Breviary. This was followed by a solemn mass, then breakfast. In contrast to my own church, there was a serious formality to the worship, which I was expected to respect. Complying with this wasn't a problem too me - I would certainly not have wished to offend anyone by being obstinate. So I genuflected before the altar, made the sign of the cross at the appropriate times and learned the *Hail Mary* and the *Angelus*.

Each day was filled with customs that were not only unfamiliar but also uncomfortable. That was good for me. Beyond my instinctive objections I learned patience and found genuine faith. I learned not to criticise what I experienced but to allow it to be a means of God's gentle criticism of me. It became clear, as I sifted my prejudices and their practices, that fundamentally this was also *my church* - or rather, that we were together part of God's Church.

I walked the streets of Knowle, as I had done during the placement, and realised afresh how insignificant and irrelevant the controversies within the Church are to the ninety percent of the population who don't regularly go to its Sunday services. It's also terribly wasteful of time, energy and opportunity. The people of Knowle, like those of my own parish back home in Oadby, were unlikely to be impressed by ecclesiastical fuss. What many wanted, was the same deeply impressive relevance that I had first encountered as a young man in Alister's ministry, that sense of all this religious talk being *for something*. Instead, we hide God and the gospel behind the contraptions of our particular tradition.

I staggered down the unbelievably steep Summer Hill, where residents chock their cars lest they slide down across the Bath Road and into the River Avon. A decade before, I had spent a lot of time understanding this area by walking its streets. Walking through urban areas with eyes and ears open is something that I have done ever since childhood. I love the way that life spills out awkwardly and unevenly in towns and cities. The mingling of private space and civic space is endlessly fascinating, disclosing clues as to the lives that are lived in them. Something sticking out of a wheely-bin, or the way that the grass between tower blocks is worn into tracks by the feet of residents. Planners prescribed routes with their tarmac paths but people refuse to be so domesticated. These erosions are as revealing as the 'proper' monuments of well-ordered squares. A town or city has the feel of something only partly ordered, partly designed, adjusted and adapted by the people that use it.

If I were raised in the country, I might have the ability to look at fields and pastures with an expert's eyes. A farmer can assess a landscape, noticing how it drains, how the soil varies, how the sunlight falls on it. In the urban landscape I am more at home and can see signs of shifting prosperity, subtle migrations, changing patterns of access and exclusion.

Across the bridge, the streets of St Philip's Marsh were quieter than I had remembered them. Being a Bank Holiday, the factories and warehouses were all locked up and their car parks, usually chock-full with the vehicles of workers from across the city, were abandoned. Curiously, the only sound was of barking dogs. I saw no people as I passed the Bristol Dogs Home, whose inmates sounded like the hounds of Hades. I had visions of a great slavering Cerberus.

To distract myself from my foolish canine phobias, I thought of the busyness of Bristol's leisure spots. While I was completely alone in this vast industrial estate, The Downs would be full of picnickers and footballers and Cribbs Causeway woud be heaving with shoppers.

Through Temple Meads I looked for a particular sign that I once spotted. It commemorates the heroism of a man who climbed a gas holder to remove German incendiary bombs that had fallen on it during an air raid. Under the blue-brick railway bridges past Victorian factories and familiar landmarks towards Barton Hill. *The Rhubarb Tavern* was still standing but the school had been completely rebuilt.

At St Luke's Church I met up with Wendy Gardiner and we sat under the porch out of the drizzle. I had spent six whole months in the community as an *Urban Theology Project* during my theological training. As a family we'd worshipped here for eighteen months.

"I asked around," said Wendy. "But nobody remembered you."

I laughed. How funny that this place had been so formative

189

and special for me but that I was wholly un-remembered. I loved the asymmetry of it.

At that time, among my peers at theological college there was not so much interest in places like Barton Hill. Many students were training in the hope of a curacy in a "significant church" in a wealthy market town or affluent suburb. While at college, they mainly worshipped in Bristol's biggest and strongest evangelical churches, usually with the explanation that, "There's great children's work here. We have to think about the kids."

They agreed, of course, with the principle that disadvantaged communities and neighbourhoods needed to be served by the Church. But somehow this came with the assumption that it would be someone else's task. They presumed that urban ministry would be a specialist area for specialist ministers. In college we spoke of *contextual theologies* for the poor, the excluded and the marginalised. But what, I asked, about the theology that's taught and learned for middle England? Isn't the affluent suburb just another *context* for theology rather than theology's natural home? Isn't all our theology inescapably contextual?

Dipping into college several times a week while being based for the most part in Barton Hill during two of the terms of my first year gave me valuable experience. I learned that the answers we reach depend not only on thinking about the most crucial questions with precision. They depend on *where* one asks the questions.

In comfortable Stoke Bishop, the wealthy district where our college was situated, the environment influenced our thinking. Wrestling with questions in a beautiful old house, with the smell of oak and library books, where the light came in across trimmed lawns and between the boughs of grand trees unavoidably shaped us. The college environment channelled our thinking. The very place suggested and constrained, reassured and confirmed, if only we could see it. By *place*, I mean not just its architecture and location but also the shared memories, the traditions, values and ways of thinking that it embodies.

Barton Hill had its own powerful and very different sense of place. If our theological college been situated in a plain industrial building among Barton Hill's tower blocks, was it even conceivable that we should have thought of God in the same way as we did in Stoke Bishop?

Wendy and I walked around the estate. She showed me what had changed. "The place is completely different now." she said. I thought how familiar it all was.

Ten years ago the very first Somali immigrants were being housed here, now they are a majority of the residents in the tower blocks and low-rise flats. There have been big physical changes too. The estate had pioneered the *New Deal for Communities* programme in which fifty million pounds was promised over ten years. This amounted to ten thousand pounds for every man, woman and child who lived there. I had been provocative in suggesting that as a benchmark, the programme should consider what the positive impact of simply handing out this amount of cash to the residents would be. If plain cash could change lives, shouldn't the *New Deal* have achieved far more?

Wendy showed me the rebuilt school, new health centre, children's playground, and lots of steel fences and security cameras. There was a greater calmness and sense of peace about the place than I remembered. Apparently a lot of the money was spent on employing local people and I was glad that it wasn't simply non-resident professionals who benefitted.

We walked and talked as we went through Lawrence Hill and into the city centre. We hugged and parted at the entrace to the new Cabot Circus shopping centre, which was bustling with customers. This was such a contrast to the French Bank Holidays I had experienced, where even Ikea closed for the day.

I walked through Broadmead, along the Quay and up Park Street, remembering the very first time we came here as a family. That first move away from our native Wolverhampton was such a big one for us all.

Up Whiteladies Road and Blackboy Hill to the Downs, and I remembered the afternoon when we joined thousands to watch the solar eclipse. I had walked here often while at college, many times during the Wednesday morning period of silence which followed David Runcorn's stimulating spirituality lectures. The Downs had been a place of thinking and praying and recreation for me.

Stopping for a 'comfort break' at the public toilets by the water tower, I saw that they bore a blue plaque in remembrance of someone:

Victoria Hughes. 1897-1978. Who befriended and cared for

prostitutes when she worked here as a lavatory attendant from 1929 to 1967.

Trinity College was all but deserted. I had arrived at the start of Reading Week. The emptiness made it easier for my imagination to populate the familiar rooms and corridors with the class of 1998. I moved through the place with a peculiar mixture of complete familiarity and the remembrance of my very first visit. Little in the fabric of the place had changed. The stairs creaked in exactly the same way. The doors each closed with a unique weight and sound, the Oak Chapel still had a distinctive smell.

I found my room in the Carter building, and chatted with the few single students who remained on site.

My walking verse for the day was Hosea 11.3: *It was I who taught Ephraim to walk, I took them up in my arms; but they did not know that I healed them.* It was quite appropriate for a day in which I was thinking so much about my learning and formation for ministry.

–

I began the day at Trinity College by breakfasting with some of the students. I was delighted to find that John Bimson, my old tutor, was at work. We chatted in his study, where our pastoral group of twelve had met every Friday morning. It was great to see him and to thank him again for his contribution to my learning. So much had happened to me in the years since I was last in one of his saggy study chairs.

From Trinity I followed the route which I used to cycle home, onto the main A4, through Sea Mills and into Shirehampton. For the first time on this *Walking Home* adventure I was retracing a homeward journey that I had made lots of times.

I paused at our old home on Dursley Road, wondering if I should knock and introduce myself. Expecting that Number 29

would have changed more than Trinity College had I was content to simply remember it as it was. I met up with Arran Huxtable, who with his parents Nigel and Trish, sister Tanya and brother Kyle had been our next-door neighbours. Arran and Jon were the same age and were in the same class at school. We had become friends with Nigel and Trish and it was a great shock when Nigel died suddenly of a heart attack. As we walked down to *The Lamplighters* pub on the muddy banks of the Avon, Arran told me about his college course and how his family were getting on. These really were old haunts and the memories came flooding back.

We walked together up to Shirehampton Infants and Junior Schools, remembering how Arran and my sons Jon and Phil would share this journey so often. Good days.

There was, I supposed, a tangential connection with my walking verse for Day Thirty Four, which came from Amos 3.3, *Do two walk together unless they have made an appointment?*

I had shared little bits of my journey the previous day with Wendy, and now with Arran. Conversation and companionship come easily when you're walking.

I walked out of Shirehampton on the old road towards Bristol, where a little plaque recorded how in the days before refrigeration, live cattle were brought along the road from Avonmouth Docks by drovers. Near the top of the hill they would pause, letting the animals drink at a pool before leading them towards the city's abattoir.

Rain started to fall on the footpath past Kings Weston House, through the parkland at Blaise Castle. It turned into a very heavy shower as I walked through Henbury and Catbrain Hill and up to *The Mall* at Cribbs Causeway.

I took a coffee break at John Lewis, where I also picked up a travel sewing kit. I had struggled for four days without a button on my walking trousers and the bulldog clip I had used as a temporary repair was almost useless.

Crossing under the M5 (the first motorway I had encountered in the English leg of my walk) I found my way carefully along the back road to Over and then Almondsbury. The small unclassified road provides drivers with a short-cut between motorway junctions. It was narrow and verge-less, making the walk as dangerous as any I had been on. The monotony of the speeding traffic was relieved by a curious looking stump of a tree. Its trunk was about twelve feet tall, a foot in diameter, and I could see the sunshine reflecting in a strangely even way on the texture of its bark. When I got closer I saw that it was made of plastic. I found an identification plate: ORANGE PERSONAL COMMUNICATIONS SERVICES LIMITED. The nearby grey equipment box confirmed its purpose as a camouflaged mobile phone transmitter.

Leaving Bristol, I felt that somehow I had begun a new phase of the journey. The city had been our home for two years and now I was heading towards the Black Country, in which I had grown up and lived for most of my life.

Crossover House B&B was a very comfortable place to stay. I dined at *The Bowl Inn* on pork rissoles and a nice pint of Brain's *Rev James*. I got talking with Simon and Martin, whose miserable conversation I had overheard as I ate. It transpired that these two sullen men were in the midst of a motivational training course, which made me wonder how buoyant their mood is normally. But as we talked they told me that on the previous Friday afternoon their manager had announced that their office was closing and that they faced a massive relocation or redundancy. What a prelude to a motivation course!

–

I breakfasted with a nuclear engineer, who was managing the decontamination of a recently-closed power station. Remembering far-off nuclear science classes from my time as a student in Birmingham, we talked of sieverts and grays as we enjoyed our food.

In planning my route between friends, I had tried to even out the daily distances. Day Thirty Five, however, was always going to be an odd one. Thornbury was just six miles north of Almondsbury, leaving me an eighteen-miler for the following day.

There was still time for surprises though. On the map, Old Down looked unremarkable. Even though it was raining steadily, the village perked my spirits somehow. Perhaps it began with the two small children cycling on the path. I stepped aside to let them pass. They smiled and said "thank you", unprompted by their mum.

There were signs of investment in the village - not

spectacular sums of money but deliberate efforts to make the place better. It wasn't a naturally attractive place but the setting was improved by some well maintained open spaces. The houses weren't anything special but this place felt as desirable a place to live as any I had passed. It had a palpable sense of community and I felt nothing but warmth towards it.

My positive feelings to the place contrasted with the sentiments of Jonah, in verses three and four of chapter three: *So Jonah set out and went to Nineveh, according to the word of the Lord. Now Nineveh was an exceedingly large city, a three days' walk across. Jonah began to go into the city, going a day's walk. And he cried out, 'Forty days more, and Nineveh shall be overthrown!'*

I wondered about the size of Nineveh. At my pace, three days walk would be about forty-five miles - that's some city.

Through Alveston, I reached my destination, Thornbury, not long after noon. I took my time over lunch in a pricey cafe, then whiled away another hour in the town's fascinating and tiny museum. It was run by volunteers and with no admission charge. I got the impression that visitors are few and the team made me very welcome.

"You will sign the visitor's book, won't you?" asked one of the ladies.

I decided to use up more time by getting a hair cut. I found a barbers with a disappointingly large queue. Most of the queuing customers were teenage boys, on half-term holiday and the barbers catered for them with a games console. The console came with just one controller, so in addition to its own sound effects, the place was filled with argument about whose turn was next. Eventually my turn in the barber's chair came and I was mauled with the roughest handling I've received from anyone armed with scissors and comb. My barber was in his twenties, his right arm was tattooed from shoulder to wrist and he moaned constantly about how little he was being paid.

He'd only just finished with the electric razor when the power failed and the lights went out. Fortunately I wasn't left with a half-finished hair cut.

"No thanks!" I insisted when he wielded a cut-throat razor for the final trim. He looked surprised but after inflicting serious pain with a plastic comb there was no way I was going to let him loose on my neck with a blade.

Mary and Roger at *Wellwater B&B* recommended *The Royal George* as a place to eat. I had arranged to meet up with Neil Cole, a close friend from secondary school, who I hadn't seen for thirty years. But first I needed to eat. *The Royal George* had recently undergone a refurbishment and was trying to establish itself as a trendy eatery rather than a plain pub. I ordered a blackened chicken linguine but was served with a salad. I took it back to the dull barman who had taken my order and almost short-changed me by a fiver.

"I ordered linguine but I've just been served a chicken salad." He looked confused.

"There's no *pasta*." I added.

"Oh," he replied uncertainly. "Is linguine a kind of pasta?"

After leaving our school at sixteen, Neil joined the army and spent fourteen years in the Signals regiment. Since then he had done all sorts of jobs, moved around the country and abroad. Recently he had been working as a civilian contractor for the British Army in Afghanistan. A father of two daughters, he also has two granddaughters - and he was only a couple of months older than me.

We talked for hours and eventually were joined by Sandra and Claire, his wife and youngest daughter. I think we were the last to leave at eleven thirty, having remembered old schoolmates, teachers and the holidays we took together to my grandfather's cottage in North Wales.

I loved the way that Neil remembered so much of the detail and couldn't believe it had taken us so long to meet again. It was exactly the kind of renewal of friendship that I had hoped for on the walk.

—

Roger and Mary gave me a filling and very tasty breakfast before I left Thornbury. On top of a couple of large meals from the previous day and four pints of beer in the evening, the fried food settled my queasy stomach. It was good to get on the road slightly earlier than usual since I knew this would be one of the most testing days. I had nineteen miles to walk. More crucially, I had to climb the southern hills of the Cotswolds.

The cloud soon lifted and I walked an easy few miles in sunshine, across the A38 and over the M5. This was the first time in the whole route that I was heading east as well as north and it felt odd for the sunshine to fall on my right side.

I turned to pass Leyhill prison, where I spent Holy Week in 2000. Julie Nicholson and I led a college "mission" to the prison with a dozen other students. It was one of the most significant parts of my training. I would have liked to go inside, to wander through the wings where we had many conversations with prisoners, the theatre where we put on a passion play with the help of the inmates, the chapel where a spontaneous Good Friday service took place, the cell where I slept.

It occurred to me that with a third of Leyhill's prisoners serving life sentences, some of those who I met all those years ago might still be inside.

My walking verse for the day was the great injunction from Micah 6.8, *what does the Lord require of you but to do justice, and to love kindness, and to walk humbly with your God.*

I bought a pork pie for lunch at the Tortworth Estate shop, chatted with assistants who were astounded at the distance I was walking and took to the road again.

The noise of the M5 was a more or less constant companion and I wondered if I might be able to slip through the trees and have a coffee at *Michaelwood Services*. I would have enjoyed being a pedestrian visitor but sadly, I couldn't find any access so it remained forbidden and off-limits.

The late night with Neil made the day's walk even more fatiguing. By the time I paused at the railway bridge I was ready for a nap but without anywhere to sit down I pushed on towards the hills and the Tyndale Monument. William Tyndale was the sixteenth-century translator of the first English New Testament from Greek texts. His legacy includes phrases such as *the powers that be, filthy lucre, the signs of the times* and *fight the good fight.* Tyndale wasn't just a gifted linguist and translator. He was active in the great reformation movement that challenged the authority of the Catholic Church and he was fearless in following the scriptures rather than its traditions. His accurate and plain-speaking rendition of the Bible included the word *overseers* instead of bishops, *elders* instead of priests and *love* instead of charity. For his defiance of Rome he was arrested in Belgium, tried for heresy, then put to death by strangling at the stake before his body was burned.

Tyndale, I was sure, would have approved of the mobile phone technology which allowed me to have a full English Bible not only in searchable text but also in an audio .mp3 format in my pocket. I thanked God for him.

Past Nibley Green, half way up Stinchcombe Hill, I stopped for a chat with a lady, across her garden wall. She kindly offered me a drink but as I had enough in my *Platypus* bladder I declined the offer. She suggested that I go left and pick up the Cotswold Way footpath. But I had already worked out what I thought would be an easier route, taking a steep section on the road and then following a footpath through the woods to Dursley. I should have listened to her advice.

I worked out long before that the natural way of walking uphill - taking slow strides - is not very efficient. It's much better to shorten one's stride and keep to a regular pace. I shuffled up the 1:4 gradient, like a cyclist in his lowest gear. It also pays not to look for the summit, one brow of the hill is inevitably succeeded by another and then another, as the undulations of the road cheat your expectations. I didn't think about the painfully slow progress I was making, I simply trudged.

I found the sign pointing along a footpath through the woods but within a hundred yards it petered out in a jumble of muddy tracks and tiny clearings. I realised it was very likely that I would miss the track that I was aiming for and end up bogged down, so I retraced my steps to the road again.

I passed an unofficial travellers camp, unguarded by a large dog sprawled in the sunshine in the middle of the road. I turned at the next downhill road, which now joined the Cotswold Way, into Dursley.

It was hard to work out what kind of town Dursley is. It looked quite substantial and its setting nestling in the Cotswolds is an attractive one. It used to be home to the Lister Company, whose small diesel engines powered agricultural machinery and electrical generators all over the world. Although production stopped twenty years ago, clones of Listers' little diesel are still made in India and are powering tiny rural communities from a range of fuels from 'proper' diesel to vegetable oil.

I had decided at the beginning of the day that the 'easy route' along the A38 and through the broad valley to Middleyard would be dull compared with the hills. Now I adjusted my route again, choosing to follow *The Cotswold Way* footpath out of Dursley but skipping an unnecessary detour over Cam Long Down.

The Cotswold Way is a well-used path. Across grassy fields, the path is worn bare, making for a pleasantly smooth and slightly yielding surface on which to tread. I briefly joined the B4066 to pass the prehistoric burial mound known as Hetty Pegler's Tump. I enjoyed cooler moments under the densest patches of trees. *The Cotswold Way* had occasionally led me through little hollows in the woods and I loved stepping into the refreshing pools of cool air.

The sun was low as I reached Coaley Peak, whose steep western escarpment is a fine launching ground for paragliders. Three of them stood on the top of the slope, taking turns waiting for the wind to strengthen, and watched by a small crowd. The breeze was just enough to inflate the brightly coloured canopies but not sufficient for a take-off. If the breeze failed them at launch at best they would have a long walk back up hill, at worst they would drop from a leg-breaking height. They looked like nervous fledglings.

Coaley Peak offered amazing views across the Severn Estuary and a view-finding board informed me that the distant dark mountains were the Brecon Beacons, some thirty-three miles distant.

The Cotswold Way demanded more of my aching feet. They bore the percussion of countless steps down and down through the beech woods. I met Bill, a seventy-two year old walker coming uphill who told me he had begun training for a walk to the top of Mount Kilimanjaro in a few months' time. Bill has walked in all sorts of amazing places, including the Himalayas. We talked about my walk and wished each other well.

The path returned to the trees of Stanley Wood and eventually I saw Amanda Ardagh-Walter, her son Patrick and black labrador Nancy, walking up towards me along the path. I had rung her husband, Nick, from the top of Coaley Peak, to tell him when I would be likely to arrive.

It was great to see each other again after about eight years. Nick and Isobella were waiting at their home in Middleyard and I enjoyed a wonderful home-cooked dinner - much of the ingredients were also home-grown - and Nick's amazingly delicious home-brewed beer. I usually hesitate in response to the question, "Would you like to try my home-brewed beer?" But for sore legs, tired mind and body the brew was a perfect conclusion to a tough, nineteen mile day.

Jennifer and I first met Nick and Amanda when they worshipped with us at Holy Trinity Church in Wolverhampton. I was delighted to hear that they still ride their specially-built tandem cycle and enjoy life to the full without a television in the house. They seemed to spend most of their time outdoors, in the garden and down at their newly acquired allotment as well as cycling and dog-walking. Time in their company is always jolly good fun.

–

Amanda toasted some of Nick's home-baked bread for me and I lingered with them until eleven in the morning before setting off.

My socks hadn't dried properly so I walked through Middleyard, King's Stanley and Frocester, dangling them from the waistband of my rucksack. Bad socks can spoil a walk but these two pairs of *Bridgedales* had been perfect. The only problem with them is that the thickness of their soles meant they took forever to dry.

The sun was getting higher and more fierce. It was humid and despite the cumulus clouds it was turning into the hottest day of the year.

At the *King's Head* in Eastington at one o'clock I had a good lunch and a pint of *Bob*. During the forty-five minutes that I was there, I was the only customer. Friday lunchtime on a hot day used to guarantee good trade and it was no surprise to hear that five pubs are closing in Britain each day.

The walk had given me a chance to survey the health of the pub trade and it certainly wasn't thriving. The quality of the food had been high - even better than I expected. A pub lunch used to mean a cheese and pickle cob but I had eaten really well in most places.

I reached Frampton-on-Severn, whose village green is reputedly the longest in the country. From the map, the walk down to the village appeared to be along a quiet lane but I had to duck into the hedges to let numerous gravel trucks and tractors pass.

It was a relief to get onto the Gloucester-Sharpness Canal at Saul Junction. The canal is broad enough to take lots of boat traffic and each road bridge could be swung to allow taller vessels to pass.

This was the first time I had walked along a canal since leaving Tancarville on Day Fourteen and it was really pleasant to have the water beside me. The biggest drawback was the heat. With the sun directly behind me, reflecting from the water's surface, I was baked.

I carried on beside the canal, swigging mouthfuls from the tube connected to the water bladder in my pack, hoping that it wouldn't run out . As I drank, a family of swans - mum, dad and eight plump cygnets came up to the bank to pose for photographs.

Eventually I decided I needed a longer break and slumped onto the grass beside another swing bridge. I unbound the laces on my boots, heaved them from my feet and stripped out the insoles so they could air in the sunshine. My tired back, neck and leg muscles relaxed and my bones sagged into the grass. I covered my head with my hat and dozed. Goodness knows what I looked like.

I pressed on towards Gloucester, counting down the mileposts. At about six-thirty, approaching the city its disused and dishevelled wharfs gave way to newly-built offices, a partially-built *Sainsbury* store and waterside apartments. Big money was being invested in Gloucester and it was good to see the docks being improved. The dockside development in the city centre was in full swing, even in the midst of a recession.

Trish, landlady at *The Spalite Hotel*, told me that the new shopping centre was being opened the very weekend that I had arrived. She wasn't sure of the name of the celebrity who would be officiating. "He's that naked Chinese man."

"Gok Wan?", I offered.

"That's 'im!"

She told me in her wonderfully broad Gloucester accent that when the centre opened for the very first time last Saturday it was chaos. "People were stuck in the queue to get out of the car park for two hours."

It was seven o'clock when I had completed the day's fifteen miles and reached *Spalite Hotel*. It's in a perfect location but at £25 a night including breakfast was very much at the budget end of my accommodation list, so my expectations were low. The drunks on the street didn't encourage me either. But the hotel was fine - clean, neat and tidy.

I was just too tired to go out to eat, so I washed and changed and ate a flapjack for dinner in bed, listening to the radio. It was great to talk with Jennifer and to plan to meet in Tewkesbury on Sunday.

My walking verse for the day was Zechariah 10.12: *I will make them strong in the Lord and they shall walk in his name, says the Lord.*

—

Four weeks before, Rouen surprised me when I found it was holding a twenty-four hour powerboat race on the weekend that I arrived. Gloucester followed suit on Day Thirty Eight by surprising me with its annual *Tall Ships Festival*.

There were just five or six fully-rigged sailing ships. But even at ten thirty the crowds around the docks were growing. I liked the steam dredger whose chain of buckets scraped and scratched so noisily that it sounded as though the whole mechanism was about to seize.

The smoke from a steam crane blew through the rigging of the ships tied up at the quay and it was possible to imagine how busy these docks would have been one hundred and fifty years ago.

I slipped away from the dock through a small path, turning into *The Glavum Way* footpath alongside the mud-brown Severn. It was hard to avoid comparisons with the Seine, which frankly makes even the fully-grown Severn look like a dirty trickle. Even the Eure, the biggest tributary of the Seine that I crossed, put the Severn in the shade.

The path led through those kinds of small land-locked urban spaces which can't be developed for lack of access. The concrete undersides of bridges and flyovers offered graffiti artists canvasses perfect in every respect, except for the lack of viewers.

Soon the path changed from dust-covered concrete to a nettle-maze. I found the track along the riverbank, where *The Glavum Way* and *The Severn Way* are one and the same path. Nettles had never been far from me on this walk but those on *The Severn Way* could win awards at the Chelsea Flower Show.

I had to lift both arms high as the most overgrown parts of the path were armpit-deep in nettles. The freshest leaves pierced my walking trousers and made my knees sore. Blue dragonflies rose before me in their hundreds as I disturbed them with each ruffling stride. It was the height of the mating season and almost all of them were conjugally coupled, in flight as well as on the nettle leaves.

I was surprised to meet two walkers coming the other way. Dave and Susan are walking *The Glavum Way* in stages, parking a car at each end of a day's walk. Susan was wearing walking shorts and asked hopefully what nettle forecast I could offer. I broke the bad news. There was a way off the path to the road but if she persevered I reckoned it would be agonising.

The pub where I had planned a swift half turned out to have become a Chinese restaurant. The staff were obviously disappointed that I wasn't a dining customer but served me a nicely chilled, and expensive, half-pint of cider.

I decided I had had enough of nettles and took the narrow lane to Sandhurst, a long strung-out kind of village. I wondered how these homes had fared during the awful floods of 2007.

At Brawn Farm I followed the bridle path to the top of Sandhurst Hill, where an inviting bench lay beneath a tree, next to the trig point. It made a fabulous place for a rest. Under the scorching sun, the hills and vales of Gloucestershire were laid out in all directions; Creation in all its beauty.

The downhill path was tricky, as the sun had baked the hoof-stomped mud into ankle-turning terrain.

At the foot of Wainlode Hill I stopped at the *Red Lion* for a late lunch. Having written on my blog the day before about the evolution of the pub lunch, it was ironic that I ate a plain cheese and onion sandwich on white margarine-spread bread. The plain food helped the taste of Wickwar *Cooper's Bitter* though, a perfectly balanced beer with a delicious toffee chewiness.

I plugged in my earphones and listened to the radio commentary on the FA Cup Final. Chelsea went a goal down as Everton scored after twenty-five seconds.

Another narrow lane took me into Apperley, a village of two halves if ever there was one. The southernmost part was a country estate village, whose cricketers played on an attractive green amidst hay-making farmers. Two machines worked in partnership. The first machine gathered and baled the hay, which had already been mown. The second picked up the bales, held and twisted them while two spinning arms wrapped them in tough plastic film. It was as fascinating as the cricket beyond.

The brick semi-detached homes of north Apperley contrasted with the south and led me out of the village towards Deerhurst.

I stopped at Odda's Saxon chapel, sitting in the cool darkness to rest and pray. It dated from before 1056 when Odda, an earl created by King Edward the Confessor, died here at the height of his wealth and power. He was apparently described in his time as "a lover of churches, restorer of the poor, defender of widows and orphans, helper of the oppressed, guardian of chastity."

I picked up the river again for another stretch of *The Severn Way*, past several gigantic oaks. The river, trees and meadows made for a beautiful walk in the sunshine.

By the time Chelsea had beaten Everton I was approaching Lower Lode, past a NO ELVERING sign. I rested at the boat club, whose wall was painted to show the levels of past floods. 1947 had been a bad year but the level of 2007 was much higher - well above my head.

The day's twelve and a half miles left me just a couple of miles short of four hundred for the walk so far.

It didn't take long to find *Malvern View* bed and breakfast at Tewkesbury's riverside. I was in the smallest bedroom yet, little bigger than my single bed. But it was very comfortable and clean. Ron and Helen made me very welcome. It was great value too - the cheapest rate of my whole trip.

The *chicken dhansak* at the local curry house was tasty, especially as I had requested some finely-chopped green chillies as a topping.

Jennifer and I spoke on the phone again and it was great to

plan a reunion on Pentecost Sunday.

My walking verse for the day was Matthew 9.5: *For which is easier, to say, 'Your sins are forgiven,' or to say, 'Stand up and walk.'*

–

Sunday - a rest from walking and, even better, Jennifer came down to meet me.

Without miles of walking ahead of me, I settled for cereal and poached egg on toast, then watched Andrew Marr interview Gordon Brown. Sunday morning television is a complete unknown to me, as I'm usually busy.

Jennifer arrived just in time for us to get across to the Abbey for the eleven o'clock service. It was a Sung Eucharist for Pentecost, and though that's not my normal preference, it was very uplifting and charged with the presence of God.

It was the first time that Jennifer and I had seen each other in two weeks, the last being with our friends in Bournemouth. And now I was just two weeks from home, not much more than a hundred miles to walk. Though my walk had been a solo adventure, and though I had missed Jennifer, Jon and Phil, I never felt lonely - the awareness of the presence of God by his Holy Spirit has been varied but unfailing.

We found a café serving roast pork for lunch, went for a stroll, had a coffee, an ice cream and a drink. We talked and talked and held hands through Tewkesbury. It was fantastic to be together again.

My walking verse was Mark 12.38 *Jesus said, "Beware of the scribes, who like to walk around in long robes, and to be greeted with respect in the marketplaces..."*

Someone asked me before I set off if I was going to wear a clerical shirt and collar as I walked. "It could be useful," he said, "people will treat you better".

Sadly, he was probably right. But it was not a suggestion that I was going to adopt.

I noticed, after I was ordained, the difference that wearing a collar made. On the street, some people smiled and acknowledged me, most were careful to avoid making eye contact. Some even crossed the road. Four days after wearing a clerical collar for the first time, I was on a Walsall pavement when a young man with a wild look in his eye walked up and punched me on the jaw.

I wear a collar most days in my normal ministry. It's good to walk the streets of the parish in a visible way. But I was enjoying being incognito during the walk, and welcomed the fact that when people were courteous or pleasant it wasn't that robes or a clerical collar had provoked their respect.

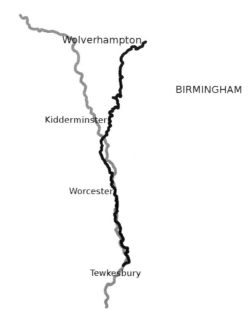

Tewkesbury to Wolverhampton - 65 miles into my Black Country homeland

Chapter Eight - Tewkesbury to Wolverhampton

Day Forty was another of my peculiar short walks. Gloucester to Tewkesbury was a convenient distance for Day Thirty Nine but trying to reach Worcester in one go would have been tough. So instead I had set my sights on Uckinghall, just south of Upton-on-Severn.

Breakfast at *Malvern View* in Tewkesbury was delicious, especially the bacon and sausage, which Ron gets from the local butcher. With time on my hands I chatted with him and Helen, a Scottish couple who have lived in Surrey, USA and South Wales. Ron worked as a technician in the textile industry and had to relocate as companies closed or moved. We talked about the decline of manufacturing and how they now found themselves in the bed and breakfast business.

I took a few wrong turns trying to pick up the river path. Tewkesbury is at the confluence of the Severn and the Avon and the smaller River Carrant. I doubled back from Telford's bridge, along the lock and found another dead end at some new riverside homes. Eventually, I got onto The Mythe, the land between the

Severn and Avon, whose flooded pumping station was the centre of so much attention during the summer of 2007. Five inches of rain had fallen in a single day and the already swollen Severn burst its banks with disastrous effect. Thousands of people were left without drinking water for two weeks and many were forced out of their homes. Tewkesbury was completely cut off for days, except for one footpath along a disused railway.

It was hard to find the right path. I tunnelled through high cow parsley and nettles but the path petered out in a small clearing. Tucked behind the overgrown weeds was an inflatable dinghy. Only for a fraction of a second did I think about taking it out onto the water for a bit of fun.

Backtracking yet again, I picked up the proper path, which led me to the pumping station. There's still evidence of the floods. The most obvious change is the new bastion built of huge sacks of gravel inside a tough plastic membrane. Each sack was a metre cube. The recently re-routed footpath led me over these defences via steel platforms and steps, into the pumping works itself, and back out again.

I followed the Severn as it turned north west, alongside large angling lakes. At one point I paused for a breather and stopped to look at the lake between the trees. Immediately, a trout leapt from the water. It rose at least a foot, flexing its body into a powerful curve, and snatched an insect from the air. It was majestic and made even more special by the fact that no one else witnessed it but me. This was the first time I had seen anything like it. I have often turned at the sound of a splash, only to see rings and ripples. But never have I seen the flat water burst by a fish like that.

I reached the end of the lake and although my map showed the footpath continuing along the river, the arrow markers on posts suggested that I had to switch inland.

I feel like a stranger in the countryside. Being a conformist and not wanting to offend against the rules, I set off away from the river. I walked around the field of green barley instead of wading through it as the map indicated I should.

I picked up a bridle path, which I figured would be more substantial and easier going than a footpath. It wasn't.

The path led to a gate, with another arrow marker pointing across a huge ploughed field. Clearly the bridle path had fallen into disuse and the farmer wasn't too bothered about preserving it. I suppose that ploughing it was easier and gained him another couple of hectares for his crop. I set out across the field, which was very heavy going. The earth was like concrete and the sun had baked it into crazy uneven shapes. I picked my way slowly under the scorching sun, dreading a slip that would twist my ankle.

As I approached the far end of the field I could see cattle beyond the gate. A few months before I would have gone straight through, albeit nervously. But a few months before I began Walking Home, someone I know was trampled by bullocks, spending two hours in a field and weeks in hospital with broken ribs and collar bone. That had led me to search on Google for "walker" and "attacked by bull". To my horror, the screen was full of stories. It seemed as though goring by bull or trampling by cows are as likely as getting caught in a heavy shower.

A dozen cattle lay in the field beyond the gate. They looked almost full-grown and were different colours and shapes. One had long horns that curled in different directions to threatening points. Were they cows or bulls? I got closer still and the nearest, a brown and white Hereford with a very heavy brow heaved himself to his feet. I looked for udders, hopefully. I was disappointed.

He fixed me in his eye. I walked to the gate. It was a narrow field - perhaps a hundred metres to the hedge of the next. Was that short enough to outrun a dozen young bulls? No way. Looking closer, I saw that there was no gate on the other side, just an opening to another field. I could have been chased right over the hill if they fancied the sport.

I considered my options. I weighed the pros and cons, even thinking that a minor goring would spice up my story. Broken ribs would be almost mended by the time my sabbatical ended.

Two more cattle, one male, one female, roused themselves for possible action. Did they look calmed by the heat? Or were they up for a fight?

I decided to retreat. That meant yet another doubling-back, this time across the wretched ploughed field once more.

I eventually rejoined the road and worked my way round the lanes. At one point I looked across a hedge through the field of cattle and the ploughed field beyond. I had added exactly an hour to the walk. It wasn't far to Uckinghall and Ivydene House offered me a sumptious welcome. I had a huge bed and en-suite bathroom, with the use of two downstairs lounges, a conservatory and vast garden.

At five, I was joined by Katri, of Ecclesiastical Insurance, one of my generous sponsors. She interviewed me for a press release and I was glad to tell her about the walk and how impressed I was with Gloucestershire. I think I might have forgotten to mention my cowardice in the face of the cattle.

I set off to *The Railway Inn*, the only pub in the village, to be disappointed by the information that there was no chef on Mondays and therefore no food. After a lunch of nuts and raisins, my dinner was nuts and crisps. And beer, of course. The Cannon Royal *Muzzle Loader* was a bit of a 'misfire' but St Austell Brewery's *Proper Job* lived up to its name.

It was good to sit at the bar and talk with the locals. Dave, who had run a plumbing wholesale business, a barmaid who loved New York but hated San Francisco, and an ex-submariner from Cheltenham. I also met Judi, who had appeared on BBC's *Midlands Today* news bulletin that evening, after moving some of her possessions back into her Uckinghall home two years after the flood. When I returned to my room, I saw her on the late news.

My walking verse was Luke 7.22 *Jesus answered them, "Go and tell John what you have seen and heard: The blind receive their sight, the lame walk, the dead are raised and the poor have good news brought to them."*

–

I lingered at Ivydene House in Uckinghall, enjoying its luxury and getting ready for a very hot day. The weather forecasters predicted temperatures as high as twenty eight Celsius so I filled my two-litre *Platypus* to the brim. It was after eleven when I got out.

Beyond the hedge of the lane I could hear voices, speaking Eastern European languages. Through the branches I saw a couple of dozen workers picking strawberries under the scorching sun.

The walk to Worcester offered a choice between *The Severn Way* and the A38, or some combination of the two. A riverside walk or a trunk road?

I decided to cover the section to Ryall on the A38, which has the distinction of being the longest A road in the whole of England. It's the old Exeter-Leeds road and the section on which I was walking once carried all the traffic between the Midlands and the South West. When the M5 motorway opened in the 1970s it left the A38 with only local cars and trucks, so I found it quiet and easy going. With buildings to look at and hedges low enough to leave the views unobstructed it offered better panoramas than the Severn Way. It even had a pavement, so there was no traffic dodging to worry about.

Before long I came up to some roadwork vehicles. The gang of workers had erected a fence of temporary barriers to divert the footpath. I stopped for a chat and they laughed while telling me that I was the first pedestrian they had seen in two weeks. I asked what they were doing and they told me they were removing old copper telephone cables, which had long since been replaced by fibre optic cables, "before someone else pinches them".

The A38 reminded me of America's Route 66, on which I drove for a couple of hundred miles one summer. Its former status as a major national highway is evident in the breadth of its carriageway - smooth cambered bends and a collection of petrol stations turned into second hand car dealerships.

I found a burger van in a lay-by and stopped for a chat and a huge mug of tea for just 60p.

The Yorkshire Grey inn once catered for a busy stream of motorists but I found a notice on the door declaring it was closed on Mondays and Tuesdays. It can't be long before the pub closes altogether. A little farther on I spotted a garden centre and restaurant. I though this would give me an economical lunch but paid an extortionate £4.50 for a plain tuna sandwich and a can of coke.

The sun was really intense but with a good walking surface and plenty to drink, I was getting through the miles easily.

I passed through Kempsey, renowned for the summer of 1841, during which a giant carrot over four feet in length was grown. Having reached the southern edge of Worcester in the late afternoon., I decided it was time to revert to *The Severn Way* and after a brief open path through a caravan park, I was soon plodding through the nettles again. It was striking how much less I could see and how quickly the river walk made me fed up.

A stream interrupted the course of the footpath. An unofficial short-cut lay invitingly in front of me in the form of a couple of fallen boughs. The drop beneath them would have left me badly hurt if I fell but I decided it was worth the risk. With my heavy backpack I wobbled onto the thick branch. Taking it very carefully, I edged forward. Confidence grew and I clambered across.

The path opened out at Diglis Lock and from here it was easy going into Worcester. It was busier too, with plenty of people out enjoying the sunshine.

I reached *Burgage House*, next to Worcester Cathedral, as the bells chimed five o'clock. Louise welcomed me at the door with a cool glass of iced water in her hand - a very kind thought. Not knowing Worcester very well I took a short walk through the city centre to find somewhere to eat. The city is full of cafés and bars but none seemed to serve meals in the evening. Finally, I sat in a cheap chicken and pizza place, with a modest chicken burger and fries. The only other customer debated with the counter staff debated, in Urdu I believe, the troubled situation in the Swat Valley in Pakistan.

I met up with my mother. After a long search we found somewhere we could enjoy a quiet drink, and we talked for the rest of the evening.

The encounter of the risen Jesus and the two disheartened disciples on the Emmaus Road is one of the best known Bible passages in which a walking journey is significant,

The incident is recorded in Luke 24.17, *And he said to them, "What are you discussing with each other while you walk along?"*

At this point, the identity of the stranger is unknown to the two disciples. They talk of their discouragement at the death of Jesus. After a long conversation they invite him to join them for dinner. As he takes the bread, blesses it and shares it with them, they realise who he is. That Jesus was with them as they ate was one thing; that he was with them on the road in their unbelief, graciously present yet undemanding, was even more amazing.

–

As I packed my rucksack yet again, it didn't feel much like my birthday. The dates by which my normal life is charted had become more or less meaningless during my walk. My forty-sixth birthday felt irrelevant. But birthday wishes soon appeared for me on emails, through *Facebook* and *Twitter*. I was very thankful.

I chatted with Louise, proprietor of Burgage House for a long time after breakfast and it was after eleven again before I got out into Worcester. On the bridge over the Severn I had a call from the *Leicester Mercury* newspaper, who want to run another story, this time about my use of *Twitter*. I hoped that I made sense to the reporter and that his readers would make sense of his version of my words.

It wasn't easy to remember all that's happened during the walk. And the deeper themes which I was exploring in relation to pilgrimage, the idea of journey as metaphor, and the solitude weren't easy to express in pithy phrases. But something else made it hard to think. The task of walking was dominating all that I was doing, so that what was before me in each moment sparkled with clarity, whereas all that was in my imagination and memory became fuzzy. This was at least partially due to the physicality of the challenge, which numbed my mind to some extent.

Before Walking Home I had wondered if I had become physically tougher, so that I would feel less pain and tiredness than I did during the months of practice. That wasn't quite how it worked out. Rather, the toughening process had simply made me *less bothered* about discomfort. The aches and pains, if I paused to think about them, were still there. If I allowed myself the opportunity, at any moment I could have identified each of them and counted them into double figures. And if I had not committed myself to the walk, I might have sat down and thrown off my heavy gear with a big sigh of relief.

The fact that I didn't fascinated me. There was something wonderful about the fact that each day's walk wasn't optional - such a contrast to the flexibility of my usual role. This was a peculiar paradox - being delivered of the burden of deciding what to do felt like a liberation. I had no choice, I had to do what I had committed to do, and that felt like freedom!

This made me wonder again about those aspects of public ministry which most fatigue me. What could I learn from the experience of walking that I might apply when it was all over? After all, a good sabbatical is not simply a break, but an investment whose dividends will make a real difference in the long term

When I consider all that I do as a clergy-person, there really aren't many tasks that frustrate or weary me. Almost all of the huge range of things that I'm involved with feel important, of some real significance to other people, and enjoyable. Even administration, when seen as an opportunity to serve people well, can be satisfying. The bit of me that likes things sorted and planned actually gets a little thrill from organising and preparing.

The tasks in themselves are therefore not a problem - I really do love what I do. But the mismatch between the number of tasks that I could do and the time and energy I have available for them - that's where the problem lies. I'm not alone in this. Talking with other clergy, I realise that all of us struggle with the same issues. The job is never done.

If we were working for the Church of England, or for our congregations or even for ourselves, the problem would not be so bad. We could negotiate reasonable targets, focus on priorities and be untroubled by what we agreed to neglect. But ministers don't work for the Church, for the people who pay their wages, nor for themselves. We live and labour for God who, we understand has called us to a pattern of being and doing in a way that corresponds to his purposes. It's thrilling to be not-employed, in the conventional sense, in order to be available for this ministry. The challenge is to keep rediscovering what shape that vocation is.

This is not just an issue for clergy. Every Christian has to work through what it means to respond to God's calling, in and through the complexities of work and family life. Through taking time in prayer and reflection, talking with others and study it's possible to confirm this calling.

In Walking Home, for those fifty-two days the shape of my vocation was wonderfully clear and straightforward. It was, I came to understand, to simply walk before God. At its most basic, this meant getting from A to B each day by the use of the feet God gave me. But it also meant getting there in a certain way, making my way properly, travelling well. "Walking before God" became for me a shorthand for living the fullness of the life God intended, in a way which enriched the lives of others.

These fifty-two days were a wonderful gift for the clarity of vocation that they provided. Through the generosity of family, church members and colleagues in my parish and in the wider church, I had the benefit of being released from the expectation of doing other things.

The precise insight that I discovered in relation to all this is that constantly choosing what to do is fatiguing. The paradoxical freedom of my pilgrimage was that I did not need to choose what to do. I had already made the choice to walk my pilgrimage long before. Now I simply had to walk it, to reach my day's destination, that was all. My daily goal was wonderfully clear. This still left me to choose a route, but deciding *how* is much more straightforward once you've decided *what*.

It's difficult to express just how liberating this was.

We live in an era when we must constantly choose *what* to do from among the impossibly huge amount that we *have* to do. This is a strange kind of freedom. Thankfully for many of us, we don't simply have to pick crops, gather hay, break rocks or operate machinery for an allotted shift. Instead, the modern employee works towards objectives, which he or she is required to complete by a specified deadline. This looks at first sight like an easier option than slogging away in unthiking toil. After all, it permits us that most celebrated benefit of the twenty-first century lifestyle: *choice*.

Yet having the choice of what to do in any given moment can be more of a burden than a blessing. The worker who is free to choose what task he does at any moment bears the responsibility not only to work well but also of ensuring that, however insufficient his time and resources, the objective is met. This is what has changed work for many people from something that exhausted them to the point of falling asleep into something that keeps them awake at night.

For fifty-two days I was toiling hard and sleeping well. It was refreshing beyond belief.

I reverted to *The Severn Way* again and walked along the west bank of the river, opposite Worcester's racecourse. Thankfully, the footpath was in a more walk-able condition than it had been in Gloucestershire, better used, broader and with a more even surface. But, as attractive as the scenery was, it was also unchanging and rather dull.

I remembered Bill Bryson's tale of his adventures on *The Appalachian Trail*. Within a hundred miles he was bored with mountains and trees and found his short excursions off the route into towns more interesting. I feel the same about the lovely *Severn Way* - good for a time but a bit same-y. No doubt this is heresy to many readers, particularly those who'd like to get onto the *Way* for an afternoon. Not me though. I had discovered how much I like to be around people, or at least the evidence of people.

There was a good crowd at *The Camp House* pub on the river south of Grimley. I sat with a deliciously bitter pint of yellow *Batham's Best*. The voice behind me sounded exactly like that of Joe Grundy from the Radio 4 agricultural soap opera *The Archers*, which is set in this part of the world.

I left the river at this point and worked my way through lanes to the A443, a busy and fast road not very suitable for pedestrians. I dangled my bright orange pennant and watched the drivers as they rounded the bends towards me. I was almost certain that I could see their eyes widen in surprise as they twitched their steering wheels away from me.

Less lucky, or less visible, creatures than me are smashed by the traffic regularly. After four hundred miles on the trail I had become a bit of an expert on the decomposition of road-kill.

Badgers, for example, have fur so thick that their corpses lie around for ages. I guessed that scavengers find them a little difficult to munch. When they turn pitch-black, their smell is at its most revolting - so pungent it lingers in an invisible putrid pool around the carcass, sometimes for longer than I can hold my breath.

Foxes, on the other hand, seem to decay much more quickly. Almost as quickly as the assortment of pheasant, pigeon and blackbird that I saw most days.

The B4194 was less busy than the A road. But it had more sharp bends and almost no verges, taking me through several narrow sandstone cuttings, where I had to stand flat against the rock whenever a vehicle hurtled by.

Another surprise lay at the side of the road in the form of a memorial to William Gladstone, three-times Prime Minister of Great Britain. It was a substantial plinth, surrounded by a lichen-covered ballustrade and shaded under the trees. It would be difficult to spot from a bicycle, impossible from a car.

Gladstone lived for many years at Astley Hall, not far from Woodhampton House, where Sally and Pete made me very welcome in their comfortable bed and breakfast.

Sue, Ed and Matt Bodnar-Smith came over from Alvechurch in the evening and treated me to a lovely birthday meal at *The Red Lion* at Holt Heath. I even had a doughnut with a birthday candle and a foot-soothing gift. We have known each other for years. Jennifer and I were at school with Sue from the late 1970s.

My walking verse for the day was John 8.12: *Jesus said, "I am the light of the world. Whoever follows me will never walk in darkness but will have the light of life."*

John's gospel is full of contrasts. His recurring metaphor of light and dark contrasts wisdom with ignorance. Walking "in the light of life" simply means not creating short cuts or diversions of our own devising but in the footsteps of our Lord, the well-trodden paths of the saints.

—

I reached Stourport and looked for signs of activity at a polling station on the day of elections for county councillors and Members of the European Parliament. It was quiet, despite the fuss about MPs' expenses that was filling the newspapers and creating speculation that voters would use the elections to register their protest.

The centre of Stourport has a resort atmosphere. It's a kind of Black Country seaside town. The funfair stands on one side of the road north of the bridge, while the other is lined with fish and chip shops, pubs and cafés. I remember childhood outings when the crowded little lawn in the park seemed ample for our ice-cream fuelled adventures. In time I brought my own family here to play, to paddle in the pool, and to walk on the riverbank.

I've seen prices steadily fall as I've walked into the Midlands. The pizza slice and chips for £1.25 offered by one pub, if not the most nutritionally balanced meal I had seen advertised so far, was certainly the cheapest.

During my walk I had enjoyed the way that local accents slowly changed as the days went by. Each dozen miles brought subtle alterations in the vowels that locals speak. But in Stourport, the changed was marked. In north Worcestershire, I had detected a hint of Brummie but in Stourport, the Black Country accent and dialect had taken over.

At the very start of the Staffs and Worcester Canal, at the top of the first lock leading from the basin, I had a big mug of tea at the *Goodnight Sweetheart* café. Gil invited me to walk through its four rooms, all crammed with furnishings, artefacts, packets and tins from the nineteen forties. It was more of a museum than a café. Gil had even wired the loudspeakers of the period radios to play band music and refitted a television set to play recordings of the 1953 coronation.

The canal walk was a real treat. While *The Severn Way* mostly afforded only glimpses of the river and felt like walking through a hedgerow lengthways, the towpath was broad, even-surfaced and gave me plenty to look at. The River Stour accompanied the canal on my right until Kidderminster, where an aqueduct allowed them to swap sides.

I crossed a rare roving bridge which was completely split by a one inch gap through the deck and sides. These were designed to allow a horse to remain harnessed to its narrow-boat as the towpath crossed to the other side.

Two young men and a young woman were ahead of me, shouting and generally being 'lairy'. I caught them up, feeling slightly unsettled in a quiet spot.

"Ay mate, am yow tired?"

"I'm okay," I smiled back.

"Om shattered."

"Why, how far have you walked?"

"From town!" (I reckoned that this was only about a mile away.) "Where yo goin'?"

I explained what I was up to, how far I had come and where I was heading.

The other youth, who hadn't done any talking up to this point, stopped in his tracks. "Fair play to you, mate."

He held out his hand and with handshakes they wished me good look.

Their lairiness belonged to the lovely exuberance of the West Midlands. I saw the same spirit in a bikini-wearing cyclist, who passed me on the towpath a few miles farther north and raised both hands high above her head as she rode on, just a couple of feet from the water.

Canals are expensive things to build. The most economical way to construct them is to keep them flat and straight. But neither is possible for long in the West Midlands. So at Cookley, the sandstone had been blasted into cuttings, and the canal twisted in tight turns. I shared the Cookley Tunnel with the narrowboat *Jamie,* as she chugged fumes and engine noise around the bricks inches above us.

Up past Caunsall and Whittington and finally I reached Kinver, where I left the canal. It was hot and humid and I had to finish the day with an unwelcome uphill walk to the very comfortable *Pine Lodge B&B*, where Anita welcomed me. It was almost six o'clock when I arrived and the day's fourteen miles brought my total to four hundred and forty-four. Just about another hundred to go.

My walking verse was John 12.35, *Jesus said, "The light is with you for a little longer, so that the darkness may not overtake you. If you walk in the darkness you do not know where you are going."*

I saw fresh significance in Jesus as the Light of the World. It's an image that's always felt somehow rather static to me. But now I realise that the light that is spoken of is light to walk by. A life illuminated by faith in Jesus is not just to be lived in a cosy glow. It's about having light to move confidently forward, instead of fumbling in the dark.

I remembered some lines from a hymn that I'd been singing for a few hundred miles:

"O let me see thy footmarks

And in them plant mine own.

My hope to follow duly

Is in thy strength alone."

—

Day Forty Four brought me wonderful reunions.

I really enjoyed the canal walk from Kinver, the "Staffs and Worcester" twisting through pretty countryside alongside the Stour. *The Monarch's Way* long distance footpath joins the towpath at Stourton and stayed with me for most of the day.

Every walker and cyclist exchanged a greeting and those on boats were happy to chat. It's a social place and I thought about how much more fun it was than the French and Southern English lanes where I was regarded with some suspicion.

I paused for a chat with Fred, who was painting the stern of his narrowboat with dark green paint that dried almost instantly in the bright sunshine. It was only after we'd been talking for ten minutes or so that I spotted a sticker in the window, indicating membership of the *Boater's Christian Fellowship*. Fred introduced me to Marion, his wife, and we talked about their recreation on the waterways.

After another hour I reached Botterham Lock, where more than twenty years before I used to sit with colleagues during summer lunch times. I worked at an electronics company on the nearby industrial estate and with only half-hour lunch breaks a trip to the pub and back was rather rushed. We would often walk up a narrow path to the canal, eat our sandwiches and enjoy the fresh air. With the bravado of young men, we found it easy to jump across the lock.

"I reckon I could do that from a standing jump," said Andy one day.

We met his boast with scoffing. "No way!"

"I reckon I could. Let me try an experiment. I'll see if I could jump the same distance on the grass."

Andy measured the width of the lock by walking heel to toe across the gate and then paced it out on the turf, using his sandwich box and a jersey for markers. He hitched his trousers, half-crouched and started swinging his arms. When he had built up enough momentum, he flung himself into the air and pushed his feet out in front of him.

It was a close thing. We were surprised by how far Andy could fly through the air. It would be harder to do it for real.

"See!" a colleague teased. "I told you you couldn't"

"Tomorrow," Andy replied. "I'll bring my kit and I'll jump that lock, you watch."

The next day we raced up to the lock again, this time Andy was wearing his training shoes and a change of clothes, just in case.

He looked doubtful as he lined himself up for the jump.

We spread ourselves around the lock, I stood on the middle of the gate, with a camera in my hand.

Andy crouched with his toes projecting slightly over the edge of the bricks, a few inches above the brown water. He furrowed his brow, took deep breaths and began swinging his arms. With a shout he launched himself upwards and forwards.

In mid-flight I snapped my finger on the camera shutter, then looked for his landing. Andy's shins piled into the brickwork on the far side of the lock and he tumbled into a heap on the concrete. We winced.

"Well done, mate!" We congratulated him with pats on the back and then inspected his bruises.

Andy's leap was pretty impressive. He'd made it almost all the way across, his toes dipped into the water as his shins took the impact. It took him three more attempts before he made a completely dry jump.

I ducked down the narrow path onto Wombourne's industrial estate and spent an hour and a half at the company where I worked for fourteen years. I was visiting on the day after the twenty-fifth anniversary of the start of my employment and it was great to catch up with lots of my colleagues who were still there.

Back on the canal to The Bratch and then onto the disused railway, whose path led me to Castlecroft in Wolverhampton.

I reached Rob and Emma's house just before seven and before long, Jennifer joined us. The four of us had been friends since they moved into a house not far from ours, on the other side of Wolverhampton. It was lovely to be altogether again, but I had found the day really tiring - probably because I was nervous about visiting my old workplace.

My walking verse for the day was Romans 6.4: *We have been buried with Jesus by baptism into death, so that, just as Christ was raised from the dead by the Father, so we too might walk in newness of life.*

–

Day Forty Five was chock-full of rediscovery and rekindled memories in my original home town.

I was born in Wolverhampton and it remained home for the first thirty-five years of my life, so its streets are deeply familiar. Yet there had been changes too - the town felt more prosperous, more at ease with itself, more positive. Of course, these were hastily-formed impressions. I may have been remembering things as being worse in 'the old days' than they really were. Yet I still had a hunch that the town I left, which became a city not long after, had gained more confidence in itself.

After leaving Rob and Emma, I walked through steady rain up to the *City of Wolverhampton College*. When Jennifer and I were seventeen, it was the *Wulfrun College*. We took an evening class in Computer Studies with some school friends and once a week we walked home together, about three miles. It was on these long evening walks, eating a bag of chips on the way home, that our friendship grew into romance.

It was only a short walk from the college to Road, and to the house in which my grandparents lived. Every Saturday morning as a small child, my mother would take my brother and me to town, then to meet my granddad at the Eye Infirmary where he worked, then to 13 Avondale Road. It was a Victorian house, overfilled with furniture, heated by strong-smelling paraffin heaters and with a long garden for our adventures.

The rain continued steadily as I walked up Newhampton Road to the Molineux, home of Wolverhampton Wanderers. Here again was a place where I had began many walks home.

Wolves had secured their place in top-flight football a few weeks before my walk by winning promotion as champions. Hopes were high for the forthcoming season and given the link between the fortunes of football teams and the morale of a town's citizens, I wonder how much of the buoyant mood that I sensed was due to the success of Mick McCarthy's men.

As I walked up Waterloo Road I first heard, then saw, a tiny band - a couple of trumpets, a drum and a glockenspiel. Through the teeming rain they marched, with scarcely anyone watching. Behind the band was a procession of steam traction engines, chugging up the incline with brown smoke swirling through the rain. Following up the rear, three or four fire engines completed the brave parade.

They worked their way through the town. I discovered the procession was part of a steam fair at West Park. After twenty-four hours of rain, I could only imagine what state the grass was going to be in after the traction engines got there.

I met up with Doreen, my sister-in-law, at the new private art gallery which she had just opened with friends. My brother-in-law Richard, and nieces Hannah and Olivia joined us.

I lunched at the public art gallery, then pottered through the Mander Centre, down Broad Street and along the Wednesfield Road. This is where I saw the most striking changes in the city - new offices, leisure facilities and student accommodation.

The Heath Town Estate, scene of much strife in the nineteen eighties, was quiet and looked peaceable. These were streets where as an eighteen year old I had gathered with friends to watch the riots. The area had suffered from very heavy-handed policing for a long time and in the wake of the Toxteth Riot in Liverpool, Heath

Town saw several nights of burning cars and running battles with the police. I found it thrilling.

Five years later Clinton McCurbin, a young man who had been at school with Jennifer and me, died shortly after police arrived at a town centre shop. The Heath Town community was enraged and accusations were made that his death wasn't accidental. (An inquest later found that he had died from asphyxiation but recorded a verdict of "death by misadventure".) The streets were once again filled with rioters and the reputation of the police reached a new low. This time, I had felt no excitement at the rioting. Instead the whole situation was wretched and saddening, an indictment of the abusive imbalance of power that many black people experienced in relation to the police and justice system. We held Clinton's funeral at our church.

Farther on, I walked past our former home in Milton Road and saw it little-changed, except for the fake stone glued to the rendering. We had been very happy in this little Victorian terraced home, in which Jon and Phil were born.

From Milton Road it was only a short walk to Cadman Crescent, where I lived from birth until I was twenty-two. Again, so familiar and largely unchanged.

Finally, I walked up along the Prestwood Road and to my brother Adam's home in Wednesfield. We went for a drink with friend Dave at *The Vine*, decorated in 1930s style, where the Black Country *BFG* is well-kept.

We declined the offer of the "cockles man", the very same visiting salesman who used to call in to the local pubs with his large tray of seafood thirty years before. To his non-amusement we would usually drown out his call of "Cockles! Mussels!" with our chorus of "Alive, alive-oh!"

Dave, Adam and I finished the evening with a curry at the *Rangamatti*.

My walking verse was Romans 8.4: *God in Jesus condemned sin in the flesh, so that the just requirement of the law might be fulfilled in us, who walk not according to the flesh but according to the Spirit.*

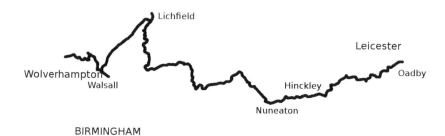

Wolverhampton to Oadby - 74 miles across the Midlands brought surprises

Chapter Nine - Wolverhampton to Oadby

Before my long walk began, I wondered what I would be thinking about during five hundred miles of solitude.

In the course of my normal life, I spend a fair amount of time planning, preparing and anticipating. So it would be natural, I thought, to get my head around the medium- and long-term future. That isn't what really happened. One of the most surprising things about my adventure was how quickly my outlook shrank to the here-and-now immediacies of every present moment. I had expected to be dis-located in space, to be moved far from the familiar. But the surprise was that I had been removed from the familiar flow of time. Perspective had vanished as I became immersed in each day's journey. This surprise was a welcome one, as it revealed how much I tend to live in my head, pre-occupied with what has not yet happened, forgetful of where I am.

But in the last weekend of my walk I noticed my attention beginning to focus more and more on the future. Revisiting the very familiar people and places of Wolverhampton wonderfully reminded me of my origins and made apparent so many changes in me. =

As I walked the towpath of the Wyrley and Essington Canal, from Wednesfield towards Walsall, I felt a deepening of an ache that has grown in recent days.

Somewhere within me I experienced a vague, unfocussed feeling that's hard to describe. None of the words that I came up with were adequate but they pointed towards it: yearning, a kind of melancholic longing mingled with compassion.

I prayed for some clearer sense of where this ache originated and slowly came to realise that I am in touch once again with *call* - what the church describes as vocation. It's that mysterious, haunting, irresistible pull that has drawn me along the road with God these past twenty years.

I should point out that none of this was depressing or discouraging. Quite the contrary, I had the sense of being energised, filled with holy discontent, counselled by the wild and free Spirit of God. It's a call I have known before, away from convenient spiritualities to something more at the edge. I had walked hundreds of miles in the gutter, along the verge. And now, in the hinterlands and marginal places of my Black Country home, I sensed something profound about these kinds of non-places.

Naturalists describe the *ecotone*, a transitional area between habitats, where species mingle and merge. Ecotones cannot be characterised as one environment or another. Ecologies exist in tension at these boundary-spaces. They are where the dominance of competing species shift. The most adaptable animals and insects, like rats and flies, use these margins as I had done, as corridors of abundance along which many miles could be covered.

I realised how much of my walk had been through the ecotones of northern France and southern Britain, between urban and rural, between public and private, between affluent and poor, between zones of contrasting ethnicity, aspiration and power. Unlike a recreational walker, moving for an afternoon through a chosen landscape, I had found my way for weeks along roads, paths and canals. And unlike a passenger in a car, train or bus, I had been radically exposed to my surroundings. The essential competitiveness of the ecotone, in which every species attempts to dominate the space, had filled my experience for seven weeks. And now, having used these hinterlands for transit I realised how much I had adapted to them. Like the towpath rat, equipped for life in the lushest of tended back gardens and the overgrown car parks of long-closed factories, I had become something of a feral creature that could live by its wits, a scavenger of novelties.

I remembered in Matthew's gospel, Jesus declared that *The foxes have holes, and the birds of the sky have nests, but the son of man has nowhere to lay his head.* One interpretation of this mysterious phrase is that it describes the general condition of all people, not just Jesus in his itinerant ministry. Perhaps my aching longing was a reminder of the essential homelessness of all humanity. Perhaps my discontented response to hearing a holy call to somewhere else echoed a deeper restlessness. This discontent and restlessness weren't bleak - they were rooted in the promise of final homecoming, which is a powerful metaphor for the fully-realised Kingdom of God. My walking home would not end in Oadby, nor in the unknown places where my ministry takes me in years to come, but ultimately with God.

–

In the gospels, Jesus is described as "being moved" in his belly in response to the needs and the quiet despair he sees. Likewise we talk of gut-feelings to describe sub-rational and super-rational insights and intuitions. I have come to know these times as significant for revelation and discovery. I was thankful that I had the time to explore them without the pressure to arrive at rapid conclusions.

My walking verse for the day brought focus: 1 John 2.6, *Whoever says, 'I abide in Jesus Christ, ought to walk just as he walked.*

"Walking as Jesus walked" - what would that involve? I decided it must include questions of place, attitude and behaviour. My canal-side route for the day led me through tough estates past back gardens and factories, literally in the backwaters of the West Midlands.

There were no pleasure boats, no scenic spots. Yet here I heard my first cuckoo since the rural forests of Normandy. I grinned stupidly.

A piano lay among the lilies in the brown water. A big black leech squirmed through a shallow puddle on the towpath. Anglers fished for carp and at Lane Head a team of convicted offenders cleared debris from a track. They wore grim, reluctant expressions and orange tabards printed with COMMUNITY PAYBACK in large letters.

It was, I thought, the kind of place Jesus walked, more like the marginal paths of Galilee than the refined districts of Jerusalem and the south.

I had also been thinking about the significance and implications of the increased vote for the BNP in county and European elections. On *Twitter* there had been a lot of outraged comment from Christians in response to the results. I agreed, of course, with these passionate rejections of the BNP's vicious racist ideology. But I was concerned that some of the righteous comments suggested a hatred towards those hundreds of thousands who voted in this appalling way.

It is a sad fact that there is a growing minority of people who feel so excluded, unregarded and powerless that the policies of the extreme right seem plausible and inspiring. The racist graffiti on the canal bridges in Leamore screamed vicious anger. What was this rage based upon and what fuelled it? I walked and wondered how simple it was to express my opposition but how difficult it felt to offer them something better - something true, life-giving and just. How do we Christians, particularly we "professional" servants of the Kingdom of God, proclaim and enact the gospel among the BNP's voters?

Jesus offended the sensibilities of the religiously-respectable by associating with the marginalised and the powerless. He brought them good news, even as he confronted their prejudice and evil.

Where should I be walking? It made me wonder, when this adventure was completed, and I would be back to work in Oadby. Which roads should I take, with whom should I travel and to whom should I seek to bring good news?

This solitary rumination ended when I reached Walsall, an unlovely but loveable town. I had a delicious plate of faggots, chips and peas for £2.99 at *Café Munchies* near the canal basin. The place was packed with shoppers from the nearby retail park. Toddlers sat in reins in their pushchairs while their mothers fed them sugary cakes. It was a glorious place; loud and boisterous and cheap. I relished the absurdly unhealthy menu, the creaky tables in the upstairs room, the huge mugs of milky tea and the attitude of the staff.

After gorging on the cheap feast I popped across to the art gallery where an exhibition offered a commentary on food. Helen Chadwick's enormous bubbling chocolate fountain was at the same time appealing and repulsive. It was a large vat of globby brown chocolate. Bubbles of air broke the surface. The oozing chocolate flopped back into itself. Having just stuffed myself to excess with cheap treats, I smiled as I let the exhibit chide me for my gluttony.

I had coffee at *The Crossing* in the heart of Walsall, where I served as a curate for three years. Paul, Mike, Tracey and Heather chatted with me and updated me on the progress of the church and its mission. St Paul's Church was built in the centre of Walsall in the nineteenth century and served the cramped streets that teemed with tenements and leather factories. Cattle would be brought through the town streets along which I had walked, from the railway sidings to the abattoir.

During the slum clearances of the twentieth century, the streets of the tiny parish were almost totally cleared of housing. Some of the better homes in The Butts and Chuckery remained. Parts of the cleared land were in-filled with blocks that soon became slums of their own. We had spent three happy years in Walsall and I still love it as a place full of gritty charm.

St Paul's Church had undergone a dramatic renovation ten years before I arrived as curate. With a massive injection of capital funds, mostly from European development grants, and an amazing vision in the church community and diocese, the building was inwardly transformed. The dark interior was stripped out, and in its place a ground floor mall of half a dozen shops were built beneath a mezzanine cafe and office floor. Above this the worship space for the church itself still had a sixty-feet high ceiling.

The stained glass windows, originally so high that they were impossible to see properly, were now visible at eye level. The tops of the nave arches made for an intriguing space. In the central lightwell, a glorious sparkling glass cross is suspended above the shoppers below, uniting all three levels in the building.

On the ground floor, a day chapel serves as a place for prayer and quiet for the centre of the town.

The investment in *The Crossing* paved a way for the redevelopment of the town, never easy in a place where political fortunes swing wildly and in which conflict is a way of life. The church community at *St Paul's* still works with the Christian social enterprise company that runs the *The Crossing* in a creative and complicated relationship. It's not easy to be the church in a setting like this. Most church members lived on the edges of the town, not in the parish. It was sometimes difficult to build relationships with the thousands of people who work and shop in the streets around *The Crossing* and who drink in the bars and clubs at night. But I loved the collision of communities and interests that made this a rich place for missionary possibility.

I enjoyed staying at Sue and Geoff Howle's home, being very well looked after and catching up with each other's lives and families. Sue still works as Church Secretary at St Paul's and it was really great to stay with them. Of all the nights on the walk, this felt like one of the highlights.

I went to see Mandy and Glyn Walker, who told me of their hopes and plans as Mandy prepared to be ordained in a couple of weeks. I remember how exciting and nerve-wracking these moments can be, and they've had a far from straight-forward journey to this point. We prayed for each other.

–

Walsall is probably one of the least regarded towns of the West Midlands conurbation. Known chiefly as the point where traffic on Europe's most congested stretch of motorway grinds to a crawl, it's a place that many people want to get past as quickly as possible. It also suffers in the mind of outsiders from the vagueness of its location. "Is that in Birmingham?", they ask.

For many visitors, the numerous towns of the Black Country merge into one agglomeration of factories, housing estates, roads and canals. But get to know the area and different textures appear. Moods and attitudes change across the region.

And I love Walsall. It has the loveliness of a town that's not trying hard to please, and mostly seems to be not trying at all. If

Walsall were a child, it would not be a pretty little thing that always behaves itself but a bog-eyed rascal that wants your affection.

At the top of the main shopping street, the newest shop was Woolworths. It was natural that Woolies would build a thriving new store in Walsall. But now Woolworths was a credit-crunch victim and its doors stayed fastened, behind hastily-scrawled notices that announced the closure.

A crowd was drawn by the *Muller Rice* promotional double-decker bus. Plenty of people were keen to pick up give-away chilled rice puddings, some to be gulped al-fresco outside Greggs the bakers. Walsall is a place where cold rice pudding causes a stir, especially if it's free.

If I found Wolverhampton more prosperous than I remembered then Walsall balanced things up. There were too many empty shops on the main road, too few bags of shopping being carried. Economically at least, things felt tougher.

Yet Walsall is good. Its people are chirpy and chatty, more likely to be laughing at troubles than moaning about them.

I turned into Darwall Street and retraced my steps of another familiar walk home. For the three years I served as curate at St Paul's Church at The Crossing, I walked this route. Every step brought back memories of a very happy period. In those three years there were more incidents and accidents than I had experienced in Oadby in twice the time.

There was the time when our drunken next door neighbour lifted a fence panel to come into our garden wielding a twelve-inch knife at another neighbour's heroin-addicted son. I leapt from my chair and went outside, hoping to be a broker of reconciliation.

"Now then guys, calm down!" I urged weakly, the words trembling out of my mouth with the same lack of conviction that I had found as a sub-prefect in our comprehensive school all those years before.

"F--- off!" said the neighbour.

It did all calm down eventually with no blood being spilt. The strife and celebration of life in The Butts continued.

When I first moved in, I found some of the problems worrisome. There was certainly quite a bit of aggression around and, while the streets felt mostly safe, life was lived with the constant implication that things could "kick off" at any time. I learned to accept it as a part of the natural order of things and in moving away, I actually missed the vitality and energy of the place. To begin with though, it led me to see trouble before it had even started.

One day I was in the back garden of our house and saw a man on one of the balconies of the upper floors of Booth House, a notorious block for short-term tenants, now demolished. He was holding something heavy in his right hand. The balcony, though some distance away, overlooked our garden. I was able to clearly see him clasp his hand in a pistol-grip. He held the weapon barrel-up, like the gangsters do when they make ready for an assault. For all the world he looked like an assassin about to take aim upon a victim in the street below.

I drew back behind the garden shed and wondered if I should call the police. I could get back into the house across open ground, then make the call. But what floor was he on? I peeped out and took another look.

Now he was holding the gun higher than before. The barrel was still pointing upwards to the ceiling above the balcony but he was stretching in a peculiar un-gangster like way. I stood and watched him as he bent down and disappeared.

After a short pause he appeared again. This time he held up a basket of flowers and hung it on the hook which he had drilled. I laughed at my absurd over-reaction.

Cars in Walsall no longer weave around the potholes, which used to appear every month outside the fire station. And the huge roundabout that some locals used to avoid in the same way that the most nervous Parisians avoid the *Etoille* is now a complicated light-controlled junction.

On the Lichfield Road I began a steady and unspectacular walk through Rushall, Shelfield, and Walsall Wood. I paused to wash down the sandwich that Sue packed for me with a pint of *Banks's Original* at The Fisherman's Rest. A sign advertised forthcoming nights of entertainment. One of the bands was called "51 Stone" and I fancied this must be the combined weight of the band members. It did raise a question though - were they a lithe five-piece boy-band, or an overweight husband and wife duo?

I shared the bar with just one other customer, a chap of

about seventy-five. We sat on adjacent tables with our pints, watching the three huge TV screens playing videos on a music channel. The show was a compilation of hits from the summer of 1981. I was eighteen at the time and during every classic hit I had to resist the temptation to sing along. But what of my companion? He would have been the age that I am now when Spandau Ballet, UB40, Genesis and Bob Marley were singing these songs. It made me wonder if I would be sitting alone in a pub in thirty years time listening to *Lady Gaga* and *The Ting Tings*. I hoped so.

In Shire Oak, in a implementation of a fabulously misguided piece of planning, the space between the swimming pool and the fitness centre had been developed as a *Kentucky Fried Chicken* restaurant. I wondered how many people used all three on the same visit.

The A461 struggles to shake off the houses that cling to this fringe of the vast West Midlands, leaving the walker who seeks the countryside to ponder "are we there yet?" for mile after dreary mile. Downhill and eventually out into the country I realised that I had given myself the problem of coping with the natural consequences of a pint of beer on a chilly day, on a busy main road with nowhere convenient for a comfort break. I began to dance the erratic jig characteristic of the barely-continent male. Finally I located an entrance to a field with hedges tall enough to conceal my relief.

At Muckley Corner I was sorry to find that the pub was shut. I wasn't looking for another drink but it was disappointing to see yet another business fail. Through its windows I could make out evidence of some last gathering. Perhaps the landlord had held a party to consume the last of the stock before locking up and walking away. It looked like a gang of revellers had feasted on the entire inventory of salty snacks and unsold bottles. A last supper, of a sort. The scene was frozen in time, leaving me to wonder if I had been looking in on the morning after the night before, or many mornings later.

Lichfield is the cathedral city of one of England's largest dioceses. It was established as the see of Mercia, covering a huge swathe of Britain, south of the Rivers Ribble and Humber and north of the Thames. Even today, after fourteen centuries of pastoral reorganisation, it's a vast and diverse diocese. Imagine the different contexts for ministry and mission in an area that stretches from the Welsh borders to the industrial towns of east Staffordshire, and from the peaks of the moorlands in the north to the heart of the Black Country.

I was ordained in Lichfield Cathedral and have attended the ordination and licensing of many friends. I have been here on conferences, courses and for meetings.

My hosts for the night were Pete and Cathy Wilcox, whose house stands in The Close, a road that loops around the three-spired cathedral and is filled with diocesan offices, the cathedral school and the homes of the Bishop and senior staff. If a television soap opera were to be set here, it would be something more than a combination of *Eastender's* Albert Square, *Coronation Street* and *The West Wing*. Pete is now Canon Chancellor of the Cathedral. But as vicar of St Paul's in Walsall he supervised my curacy and his generous training enabled me to take my first faltering steps in ordained ministry. I owe him much.

By a curious coincidence, Pete was preparing for the launch of his latest book, *Walking the Walk,* in the week that I visited. It's a dramatic re-telling of the story of David, King of Israel.

If ever there was a man who wandered from the pathway, it was David. A hero, musician, prayer-poet, inspirer of a nation and wise leader, he was also deceptive, adulterous, cowardly and a murderer. One of the most remarkable aspects of the Bible, is the frank way that it depicts men like David. It is literature that is unafraid to be critical, even of the most central human characters. A compelling part of its genius, even for those who are irreligious, lies in the way that it refuses to legitimate earthly power. A community which shapes its life in a way that attends seriously to the scriptures, will never suffer totalitarianism.

I shared a fabulous evening with Pete, Cathy, Jon and Tom and I slept peacefully, despite noticing a locking bolt on the outside of my bedroom door. I doubted very much that Pete and Cathy ever lock their guests in at night and assumed that they inherited the arrangement from a predecessor. How peculiar to think that some ecclesiastical dignitary had once made a habit of locking a family member in their bedroom.

My walking verse for the day was 2 John 1.6: *This is love, that we walk according to his commandments.*

Love then, not in its romantic sense but in the world-changing gospel-sense, is not about words but actions. And if love is walking in obedience to Jesus' commands, then it's active, simple, demanding. It is walking the walk, as well as talking the talk, of being a disciple. Thinking once more of David and his failings and his faithfulness, I slipped into sleep.

–

As I lay in the drowsy semi-wakefulness I realised that I had begun Day Forty Nine of my adventure. Seven weeks of pilgrimage. One of the surprises which arose from my experiences was how the Jewish scriptures had felt more significant than I had expected. Perhaps there was something fundamental about my exile from home and my exodus that resonated with the Old Testament.

The Exodus of the Jewish nation is celebrated at the feast of Passover, which Jesus shared with his disciples just before his arrest and trial. It was an occasion for one of the three annual pilgrimages to Jerusalem. Forty-nine days later, a "week of weeks" after Passover, the Festival of *Shavuot* marked the giving of the *Torah* or written law by God to Moses. Shavuot was also an occasion for pilgrimage, as the gift of the law marked the essential basis for the relationship of God and his people. Those forty nine days in between the two festivals are counted off one by one, in preparation and anticipation for the great event.

A similar idea carried over into Christianity, where there are forty-nine days for the celebration of Christ's resurrection at Easter. For Christians, Easter corresponds with the liberation moment of the Exodus, and Pentecost marks the basis of a new relationship between God and his people, not resting on the law given to Moses but on the gift and ongoing presence of his Holy Spirit.

At one stage in my planning I had thought about walking for forty-nine days between Easter and Pentecost to make this an especially significant season. But I needed to be in my own church on Easter Day and it would have been very difficult to prepare sufficiently to make a start on my journey the very next day. Instead, the forty-ninth day of my pilgrimage began on the eleventh of June. Unlike parts of the church, I wouldn't be marking the feast of *Corpus Christi*, which was celebrated on that date. Instead, I mused about our need for seasons.

Contemporary life is timetabled in weeks and years. We seem to have forgotten how to mark out seasons in the way that our forebears did. For teachers, students, and families with small children, academic terms and the long summer holiday is about the closest we get to a seasonal pattern for living. I've come to recognise that for me life needs a bit more shape than this. In a climate as variable as ours, progress through the seasons of weather isn't at all smooth. Most of us have forgotten to notice the waxing and waning of the moon and we commonly hear the lament that "seasonal vegetables and fruit" means very little these days.

As I lay awake I wondered how I might be more seasonal in my approach to work. I remembered how many of the ancient seasons of the calendar marked off periods of between four and seven weeks - Advent, Epiphany, Lent, Easter being the principal ones. Would a renewed seasonality be a gift that the church could offer a season-less world?

Tom left early for school so I chatted with Jon about his A levels before breakfast. We agreed that the breadth of knowledge they demand makes them the toughest part of the education path. I keep thinking about my own son - another Jon - taking his A levels at the same time. I had been worried that my disappearing from home might make it more difficult for him and for Phil, my youngest son, taking his AS level exams.

Pete and Cathy were very encouraging about my hope of turning the story of this adventure into a modest book. Their writing is so compellingly good and it was very helpful to hear their thoughts. I had been keeping an online journal of my adventures as a first draft of the book you're reading now. The discipline of writing an account of each day was helpful in lots of ways.

Before I left, Pete returned from a schools event in the cathedral and we said our farewells. I visited the cathedral itself but was probably too wrapped-up in my own thoughts to make the most of the visit. I wondered how many pilgrims had made their way to the shrine of St Chad through the centuries.

The A461 had bored me during the previous day, so not fancying the direct main road route to Sutton Coldfield I picked up the lane to Wall, once a significant small Roman town with the name *Letocetum* but now a bypassed village. I trod the main street that once bore the feet of legions. In the twentieth century, the first generations of motorists also used Watling Street as the main route between London and the Midlands. The A5 trunk route was soon diverted around Wall and, in the last decade, has itself been superseded by the M6 Toll road.

I popped in to the *Trooper Inn* for a pint of *Abbott Ale* and an incredibly cheap lunch. My large steaming plate of chilli and chips cost me £2.

Lee, the *Trooper's* manager, has what you might call an aggressive pricing policy. All starters are £1, main courses £2 or £3, and desserts £1. He had only had the place for nine weeks and I wished him well. The pub's customers seemed mainly to be Lee's friends, rather than locals. And without the prospect of passing trade, I feared that his inn might well join the ranks of closed hostelries that I had trudged past over the course of my walk.

The remains of *Letocetum's* bath house and its hostel are uncovered and open for visitors to wander around. It must have been forty years since I explored them as a child. Frankly, the remains aren't tremendously impressive, amounting to little more than knee-high footings of walls. It needs a good deal of imagination to visualise how the site would have been.

South of Shenstone the skies darkened and I began to think about rain. Timing the moment at which to pull on the waterproofs is an art in which I had prided myself. It was still quite warm and I held out for as long as I could. Still, I realised, when the rain did come it would be in a swift downpour.

I saw lightning strike the TV transmitter mast in the distance and more rumbles of thunder approached. I past a field of cows as the wind began to blow stronger. They jostled each other into the corner of the field and began to moo anxiously beneath tossing branches.

It still wasn't raining and I reckoned I could make it to the next group of dense trees before getting dressed for the inevitable downpour.

The rain started just at the predicted moment and I pulled my waterproofs out of the rucksack and wrapped it in its waterproof cover. I tried something new - putting on the hood of my rain-jacket underneath my hat. It worked brilliantly and I was spared the nuisance of water running down the back of my neck.

The storm intensified in minutes, the water running down the edges of the narrow lane getting wider and deeper all the time. It wasn't long until it became one rushing torrent, sandy brown with the soil washed from fields. I splashed through it, dangling my strip of orange fabric in the hope that any driver would see me.

I counted the delay between the flashes of lightning and booming thunder. Five seconds, then three seconds and then two. That meant the strikes were grounding about half-a-mile away. Above me hung mains electricity cables. Was it safest to be near them but not under them, so that the earth wire could divert any nearby strike? As a former electrical engineer, the question needed some thought. If I stood directly underneath them, there was a risk that I would be hit by any falling live wires. I thought that if I stood nearby, the lightning might be drawn to the higher wires than to my head.

Thankfully the storm passed over before my theories were verified and I was left to contend with the steady rain.

I reached the A5127 north of the *other* Watford Gap, less famous than the Northamptonshire village and its eponymous motorway service station. Through the swirling downpour I saw a cyclist standing on the narrow pavement, his bike lying at his feet. I crossed over to see if everything was alright.

"You okay?", I asked.

"Them am soaking me on purpose!" he pointed at the racing traffic. "They're laughing at me every time."

"What's up with your bike?"

"I got divorced, see..."

It struck me as an odd way to begin an answer about his mechanical troubles but I tried to be sympathetic. "I'm sorry."

"She 'ad me car, so I bought me a bike. But it's stuck in top gear. I'm soaked - and them buggers am laughin'."

The poor chap was suffering the breakdown of both a marriage and a bicycle. Now he was the victim of malicious splashing. It never rains, I thought.

"Sorry. Is there anything I can do?"

"Nah y'alright, me mate's gunna bring 'is van."

I wished him all the best, wondering if I could have perhaps fixed his gears with my *Leatherman Micra Multitool* (which so far I had deployed only to open one bottle of French cider and a packet of salami). Never mind, at least I had stood with him briefly in saturated solidarity.

I stood on Chris and Alison Mytton's doorstep looking as bedraggled as I had at any time on the journey. But a hot shower and a glass of *Campo Vieja Rioja Reserva* improved things considerably.

For dinner Alison had cooked a delicious tangy chilli-con-carne. It may have been my second chilli of the day but it was very welcome!

My walking verse was 3 John 1.34, *I have no greater joy than this, to hear that my children are walking in the truth.*

—

Fifty days in!

Chris and I used to eat frugally as students. We studied together at *Birmingham Polytechnic* (recently re-branded as

Birmingham's City University) and mostly lunched on cheese and pickle sandwiches. Now he was cooking us bacon and quails' eggs.

He assured me that they were left-overs from a dinner party, rather than being a regular breakfast choice. We had three each, peeling their ever-so-slightly rubbery shells and eating them whole.

I happened to mention this treat on *Twitter* and received the response, "How typically Sutton Coldfield!" from one of my followers.

Technically, I was in Four Oaks. But this is still a district that Brummies poke fun at for its middle-class peculiarities.

I set off past the supermarket (Waitrose, of course), through Mere Green and Roughley, and under the M6 Toll road.

I had been planning to reach Middleton via an appealingly straight east-west lane. However, when I studied the map, I saw that the M6 Toll motorway and the recently-diverted A38 had chopped the road into pieces, giving me a tricky bit of manoeuvring to find the right route. Jennifer rang and we chatted as I walked. But unable to concentrate on more than one thing at a time, I passed the turning that I had wanted.

I decided to take a more northerly route towards Drayton Bassett, where I spotted the *Heart of England Way* long-distance footpath running along the towpath of the *Birmingham and Fazeley Canal*. The sun was shining and I anticipated a lovely easy-paced stroll.

An hour after this casually-made decision I was neck-deep in undergrowth. The map showed that I had to reach a path which ran for half a mile on the opposite side of the canal to the towpath. The Ordnance Survey showed it clearly - a crisp red dotted line on a clean white background.

To begin with, the path was easy, following a farm track to a copse and a pool, signposted, "WARNING - NO FISHING! YOU HAVE BEEN WARNED". The letters of the word "you" were in blood red for chilling emphasis. Clearly, the sign writer had given thought as to how his words could be as menacingly terse as possible. Earlier I had seen a sign about parking outside flats in Sutton Coldfield which began almost apologetically, "POLITE NOTICE - PLEASE DON'T PARK ON THE DRIVE".

I trotted past the pond and along the field edge, checking the blinking red circle which appeared on my phone's map display, once it had locked onto half-a-dozen GPS satellites. Sure enough, I was on track.

The crop was waist high and I trod the margins through which my legs were lashed by damp barley, nettles and brambles. I had to go slowly, as if paddling through opaque seawater along a rocky shore.

Eventually I reached the end of the field at the embankment of the canal. I had to cross a wide ditch using the beams of a bridge, whose timbered deck had long since disappeared.

Up onto the canal and things got even worse. There was the barest hint of a path, just enough evidence that someone before me had also walked this way. I stooped beneath branches, walked through bulrushes taller than me, strimming the nettles with my legs, which soon began to burn.

Eventually, I reached the bridge which carried me to the towpath on the other side. An "information board" welcomed me to Middleton Quarry which, it proudly announced, was being developed as a nature reserve. "There are two footpaths," explained the sign, which also mapped the route I had battled through, "but these are not way-marked and in places, impassable. You are advised not to use them." I felt a greater ire towards the makers of this particular sign than towards the other two I had seen that morning.

I was tired, filthy from the waist down, and I still had ten miles to walk. The canal led me past Kingsbury Water Park, through the broad and shallow valley of the River Tame. This area is unfamiliar to me, though I had lived almost all of my life within one hour's drive of it. Tamworth has never appealed to me for some reason, though it's probably a lovely place. I have a grumpy and irrational prejudice towards this corner of the English Midlands where the edge-lands of Staffordshire, Warwickshire and Leicestershire connect.

Things improved from an aesthetic perspective, as I climbed the gentle hills eastwards. But I grew more and more tired until I finally entered that zone where, hypnotised by the rhythm of my walking, the miles passed beneath my feet.

My feet, I should point out, were in remarkably good nick, considering the punishment to which I had subjected them. They had accustomed themselves to the demands of hundreds of miles of tarmac without turning into calloused hooves. Soft and strong, by the time I had reached Warwickshire on Day Fifty they had borne me five hundred miles.

The soles of my wonderful *Merrell* walking boots, however, were beginning to show their wounds. In several places, their *Vibram* layers were worn thin. I reckoned that they still had at least a hundred miles left in them. Not bad, considering that with all my preparatory walks I had probably done a thousand miles in them already. Wow, I thought. A thousand miles of walking in a year! I remembered Paul, my churchwarden, who had kindly donated the cost of buying them.

I had picked up a Cornish pasty in the tiny general store in the village of Hurley, so when I reached *Abbey Farm*, near Merevale on the outskirts of Atherstone, I told Malcolm and Jenny that it was unlikely that I would emerge from the room.

The bed was huge and gloriously comfy, the bath deep and

the room generous in every way. I could have stayed there a week.

I had slipped into an hour's apres-pasty sleep before rousing myself for a couple of phone calls. Then, long before nine-thirty, I was sleeping for the night, thankful and thrilled that I had completed five hundred and ten miles and only thirty remained.

My walking verse for my fiftieth day was Revelation 3.4, *Yet you still have a few persons in Sardis who have not soiled their clothes, they will walk with me, dressed in white, for they are worthy.*

Taken completely out of context, it spoke to my bedraggled state and filthy attire. Pilgrims, I imagined, always hope that their trials deliver some kind of purification and cleansing for their soul, if not for their apparel.

–

On Day Fifty a missed turn caused a re-routing that led me into a tangle. But Day Fifty One's change of plan paid dividends.

I had thought of walking through Atherstone and then Fenny Drayton and Stoke Golding. But as I approached the Coventry Canal on a perfect day for walking, I chose to go off road.

Canal walking has been one of the wonderful surprises of this walk and I had thought that I had done the last of it in Staffordshire. The map though, showed the Coventry Canal twisting along the contours and sure enough, the scenery was surprisingly attractive.

It must have been the height of the gnat season. On the previous day, every stride through the undergrowth raised scores of them. On the canal, they flew in looping flights across the water and back. Perhaps it was the angle of their wings in the bright sunshine that meant those flying from right to left were more visible. The effect was to make them look like a constant one-way stream, matched in speed and course like a shoal of fish.

Among the notices alongside a lock I spotted a British Waterways sign about fishing. In English, Polish and Russian, it warned that fish must not be taken away but must be returned to the water. I wondered what confusions had made this clarification necessary and whether east-European families, newly settled in Warwickshire, were dining on Coventry Canal perch and roach.

A single cygnet swam with its parents. It was still grey and fluffy but chicken-sized. I fancied that like a schoolboy in juvenile shorts it wanted a grown-up outfit soon. As it passed I noticed it was swimming with just one foot. It stretched its right leg behind like a limbering athlete and I thought it would resume two-legged swimming. But it stowed the right leg among its feathers and carried on. Curious.

I enjoyed a splendidly bitter-sweet pint of *Everards Original* at *The Anchor*, Hartshill. The table next to mine was occupied by two couples, whose canal boat holiday was apparently coming to an end. They laughed and teased and shared their in-jokes. It was a cheerful conversation to eavesdrop on.

With a few more miles walked I paused for a breather on a short flight of steps at Bridge 33. A man with a dog turned up the same path and we fell into conversation. Dave was a retired local planning officer and knows this land intimately. I confessed my ignorance and low expectation for this part of the walk, which happily had been confounded.

Dave added his opinion to the claim for the Battle of Bosworth which locals have. He told me that while no archaeological evidence has been found for any site there is a letter in which the king promised recompense to four parishes around Mancetter "for my recent battle".

We talked of railways and roads, watched curious activity in the fields where some kind of targets were being set out, and wished each other a good walk.

As I entered Nuneaton, I left the peaceful canal at the moment when a radio on a construction site blared the nineties' hit *Gangsters' Paradise*. It made me smile and this was broadened when one of the first cars to pass me had, *A town called Malice* blasting through its open window. Nuneaton had introduced itself.

The sign marked ABBATOIR led, appropriately enough, to a dead end. So I dog-legged back to the main road. This featured one of the best pieces of 'roundabout art' of my walk. A tall pole was crowned with pipes which left it at all angles. Each was capped with a flat nozzle and the whole thing was showering water under high pressure. Its effect was to create a huge dandelion-head, which shimmered and shed its spray in the sunshine. Quite beautiful.

The centre of Nuneaton was as anonymous and unattractive as I had predicted. I wondered why a local bus carried the name *Larry Grayson* in large letters. Sure enough, Wikipedia confirms that he grew up in the town, under the name William White. Perhaps each bus is named after a Nuneaton celebrity, I thought. I dismissed the idea on the basis that an insufficient number of famous Nuneatoners exists for even a modest fleet.

I also wondered what it was like to drive the *Larry Grayson* bus and how many times each day passengers would shout out, "Shut that door!"

I had remembered Grayson's never-seen friend Everard. Was he named after the Leicester brewery, whose signs were everywhere in Nuneaton?

The posher end of Nuneaton, I discovered, is the east. This is contrary to most towns, where the prevailing winds privileged the westernmost houses with cleaner air in the coal-burning era. I wonder why Nuneaton bucked the trend.

A gang of youngsters in a car sounded their horn and jeered at me. I called back - nothing rude, of course. But they were clearly surprised that I should say anything. When I caught up their car at the traffic lights, I wandered across to them. The ruffian who had called out something that highly amused his friends became a bit sheepish when I appeared at his open window. So I smiled and said hello. They wound up the window and drove on, perhaps fearing that I was a dangerously calm psychopath who was unfazed by their joshing.

I finally walked into Leicestershire as I crossed *Watling Street* for the first time since the village of Wall.

Hinckley brought no particular blessing. I paused to buy a sandwich at a supermarket, which I ate on a bench outside. In towns like this, where nothing much happens, stories of local heroes become somewhat embellished. The legend of Richard Smith is a case in point.

In 1727 Smith joined a crowd in the Market Place that was gathered around a recruiting sergeant, who frightened the citizenry with tales of what might happen in Hinckley if the Papists came.

Richard, by all accounts a fair-minded chap, protested that not all Catholics were bad men, raising the sergeant's ire.

The sergeant screamed,"You ought to be defending your king, country and religion. You should be proud to fight for King George. Why, even your public house is called The George so that people might drink his health."

"Oh no," Richard shouted back, "it's called The George after St George who slew the dragon."

This was too much for the sergeant. Lowering his halberd he charged straight at Richard, impaling him on a tree.

Such a brave stand, on behalf of the Catholics and in the

cause of accurate pub-onomastics, earned Richard this inscription on his tombstone:

A fatal halberd then his body slew, The murdering hand God's vengeance will pursue, From earthly shades though Justice took her flight, Shall not the Judge of all the world do right, Each age and sex his innocence bemoans, And with sad sighs lament his dying groans.

According to the local history pages of Hinckley's community website, every April "strange red drops of moisture appear on the stone and trickle down over the inscription as if crying tears of blood for poor Richard."

I was getting tired by now and the narrow verge of the busy road towards the M69 made for more frustration. After the motorway roundabout, it was easier to relax into the simply-walking zone and to trek mindlessly towards Stoney Stanton.

Keith and Linda let me in to *The Dive Inn*, whose name referred to the nearby Stoney Cove diving centre. I had expected a pub but the *Inn* turns out to be a guest house, with overflow accommodation in the form of a caravan in the back garden. They made me very welcome and were interested in my walk.

I set off for the nearest pub for dinner but the smell from the fish and chip shop was irresistible. Perched on the bench outside, eating my dinner with a small wooden fork, I was joined after a few minutes by three lads who came out with their food. They hung around for a moment, clearly disappointed that I had nabbed their seat. I shuffled up the bench and invited them to join me and we got talking.

After a while we introduced ourselves by name and Adam, Will and Alex fired question after question about my walk. "What you doing it for?", "How much money are you carrying?", "Where's your luggage?", "How many clothes have you got?"

They told me about Stoney Stanton, which they were pleased

to call home. I heard that there's a lot for them to do, there aren't any real chavs and that it's better than Earl Shilton. This last detail seemed very important to them.

When I said that I was going to be heading off in the morning they insisted I should stay until Saturday afternoon when the Stanton Carnival takes place. I had to apologise and explain that I want to be home.

They wanted the address of my blog and for me to take a picture of them. I promised them a mention in my book.

My walking verse was from almost the very end of the Bible, in which a vision of a new Jerusalem is described. Revelation 21.24, *The nations will walk by its light and the kings of the earth will bring their glory into it.*

–

Lying awake in the neat bedroom at the *Dive Inn*, I pondered the significance of this, my fifty-second and final day on the road. The last week had rushed by. Walking through so many places I knew well was creating the impression that my journey had sped up. Compared with the weeks of exploration in France, where every bend in the path brought me to a view I had never seen before, the last week had been full of the familiar. And being with friends meant that I had had less time on my own. I had loved the reunions, of course, but without realising it, the sense of being on a solitary adventure had disappeared somewhere in Worcestershire.

Thoughts turned from the journey behind me to homecoming. I was so much looking forward to being home - a destination that I could now measure in hours. The closer I was, the more intense the longing.

I had been asked several times if there have been moments when I wished it was all over. I fully expected that there would be, that when I was exhausted or bored or lonely, I would wonder why I planned such a daft enterprise. But honestly, there weren't any.

It had been an adventure unlike anything I had done before. I had seen so much, met many interesting and inspiring people. There had been thrilling moments, times of elation and of exhaustion. I had walked happily and fearfully. And for every mile of it I've had been in solitude, but never really alone.

Jennifer, Jon and Phil had been in my thoughts and my heart all the way. Through the blog, *Twitter* and *Facebook* I remained stitched into the communities to which I belong.

And in a strange, mysteriously quiet way, I had always known the company of God. The image of the perfect completion of creation in Genesis is of a man and woman walking with God in the garden on a cool evening. Nothing is said. Not much happens. Just walking.

In Jesus, the possibility of a restoration of this relationship was given as a gracious gift. I had known the reality of this for the second half of my life, and the last fifty two days confirmed it.

I worked my way through the whole Bible in "walking verses" but chose to break the pattern for my last day and use the great homecoming story of Luke 15. Jesus tells the parable of a father with two sons. The eldest dutifully remains at home while the youngest has the audacity to take his share of inheritance and goes away. Many retellings of this story focus on the wild living of the prodigal but for me the most shocking aspect is that he asks for his inheritance while his father is still alive. It's not just that he goes his own way, it's that he wishes his father weren't still alive.

Chasing a fantasy of a better life far away, he falls on hard times when famine strikes. He comes to his senses and realises that his survival depends on his return. But even as he retraces his journey, the prodigal doesn't try to come *home.* That would involve the restoration of relationship. Instead, he plans to return to the place of his former life but with a different status, to be as a servant, not a son. He plans to be re-located, but not restored.

The twist in the story lies in the father's reaction. We might think that he would be furious or rejecting of his son. Instead, we find him running out to find his child as he makes his way back. The father seizes the initiative, rejects the idea of a different relationship and accepts his son back. His homecoming is celebrated with a change of clothes and a lavish feast.

In one of the Church's post-communion prayers we interpret this parable in the light of our renewed relationship with God: *While we were still far off, God met us in his son, and brought us home.*

The whole of my journey had been a homecoming. I had been homeward-bound for seven and a half weeks. Several times each day, I had checked my map or the position of the sun, and looked to the point on the horizon over which home lay. This journey was more than about being physically relocated, it was about experiencing the separation from family, friends and role and then allowing myself to be drawn back ever closer to them. Later in the day I would be under the roof of my house and in the company of loved ones.

This physical journey corresponded to the spiritual journey of the last twenty three years. I am walking towards home, as best I can, with God.

One last cooked English breakfast one last routine of packing my rucksack. Then I was off.

I crossed the railway line and headed up the steep road along the northern edge of the huge granite quarry at Croft. Croft Hill rises about two hundred feet above the plain of the River Soar but half of it has disappeared and a vast, steep-sided hole has been excavated. Warning signs discouraged exploration. Besides, I wanted to be back home.

I trudged on, musing on the unglamorous aggregate from places like Croft that I had trod for so many miles. I remembered the gravel from the Seine, the limestone of Normandy and the chalk of Dorset.

Friends at St Paul's Church in Oadby had asked what time I would be back and let on that they were planning a homecoming reception. I was really looking forward to it and didn't want to be late. This was the first day of the whole journey where I was working towards a deadline.

With time on my hands, I decided to make a diversion in Huncote, to see if Sue was home. She's a friend from St Paul's and I thought it would be fun to surprise her. I found my way round to her house and rang the bell. No one was home.

Through Narborough and into Littlethorpe, where I stopped off at *The Plough* for a pint of *Everard's Original* (brewed in Leicester) and a sandwich. I was counting down the miles into single figures now.

Then it was under the M1 motorway and through the site of the vast GEC factory at Whetstone. This industrial village was where Frank Whittle built and developed some of his first jet engines. Until a decade ago, it was also the place that *Dr Marten's* boots were made. The factory site included a derelict sports and social club, playing fields as well as offices and large sheds. I mourned for industrial Britain.

Glum about the state of the economy and the scarcity of manufacturing jobs I suddenly felt tired. Too much introspection perhaps. And on a hot and humid day, with a pint of beer inside me, I lost concentration. Less than ten miles from home I got lost.

I had wandered up onto a housing estate and found myself stranded on the wrong side of the Blaby bypass. The roads of estates built in the eighties and nineties aren't designed for through-routes. Instead, they offer little nooks and drives where every home is off the beaten track. I tried a couple of unpromising cul-de-sacs, hoping that they would offer me an alley under or over the bypass. They frustrated every attempt and I resigned myself to retracing my steps all the way back to a more significant road.

I worked my way eastwards, along the lane that runs over Blaby Hill, where families were enjoying a Saturday afternoon stroll. A couple of burnt out cars lay on the path. Crossing the Grand Union Canal I reached South Wigston, another industrial village-turned-town. Again, it's a story of one-time prowess now faded. They used to make bricks, footwear, hosiery, electric vehicles and drums (the musical variety) in this railway town. Now the place makes little more than biscuits. South Wigston has a reputation of being a tough district but I've always enjoyed the place. The Victorians conceived it as a model town, with a thought-out street pattern, hundreds of red-brick terraces and a planned development. It still has a strong sense of character. I like South Wigston.

I walked up into South Wigston's older sibling, Wigston Magna. I had promised to be back home for five o'clock and still had time to spare so I joined the shoppers for a cup of coffee in the *Subway* sandwich franchise.

On the way out towards Oadby, I remembered June. On several occasions during the year before my walk, my practice walks had taken me along the Wigston Road, not far from her house. She had scolded me for not dropping in for a cup of tea with her. Today, I thought, I would make amends.

Like Sue in Huncote in the morning, June was out. I laughed and wrote her a note, which I pushed through her letterbox: "I've walked to your house from Paris and you weren't in!"

The tower of St Peter's Church came into sight and I really did feel that I was nearly home. I walk this route several times every week, so I was joining my epic Walk Home with all those little, everyday walks home. At the church there was a small welcoming group who had chosen to walk the last mile with me. Jon and Phil, my sons, came to the front of the crowd and we hugged. I shook hands with all the others, declined the offer of kind friends who invited me to let them carry my rucksack, and we set off together.

They wanted to know how I was and there was so much to tell.

It took fifteen minutes to reach Hamble Road, where a large crowd stood outside St Paul's and cheered, waving flags under a big banner, "Welcome Home Simon!"

It was so good to be back.

Chapter Ten - Home

By the time I reached home, I still had a month before returning to work. I had wondered whether the habit of walking had become ingrained to the point of necessity, or addiction. It had not.

In the weeks that followed, I noticed how easy it was to return to familiar patterns of living. The context and situation in which we spend our time shapes the way we live more than we realise. Being on the road was so different from my usual experience, that I would have to think consciously about preserving its legacy.

In terms of my physical health, I was more fit than I had been for years. I lost some weight, though not as much as I had predicted. The changes were more noticeable in body shape than overall mass. My legs had become strong and I carried little fat from the waist down.

I noticed how easy it was to tackle stairs and that a brisk twenty minute walk no longer left me breathless. But walking without a rucksack felt like a different kind of exercise and I had to adapt to a different way of balancing.

My posture had improved greatly. Carrying a total of twelve kilogrammes for over five hundred and thirty miles had made my back strong and I stood taller than I had before.

My feet were in good condition too. The soles were strong and muscular but the skin was soft and healthy. I had heeded the warnings of other walkers that feet need to be treated with tender care and I trimmed my toenails at least once a week.

I was very thankful for the way that my body had coped with the challenge and knew, that if I had to, I would be able to walk fifteen miles a day indefinitely.

This had been a significant point of learning. My body was stronger than I had imagined and was capable of adapting to a rigorous regime. In fact, a lifestyle which involved six to eight hours of physical activity each day seemed to be better for my physical health than my usual sedentary one.

Beyond the physical changes, I had come to discover new things about myself, about God and about the world in general.

I had wondered about the way that I would cope mentally with a largely solitary experience. I was surprised about the way that I adjusted to simply accept the circumstances. The pains and discomforts that came from the physical demands of the walk were accompanied by psychological pains too. I missed Jennifer, Jon and Phil. I missed my friends and my work. But somehow it was possible to simply acknowledge these and get on with the task of walking. I learned that I was more adaptable than I had imagined.

My faith wasn't boosted by any especially profound supernatural experience. But it grew through constant revelations of God's grace and goodness. Providence is not so much a popular idea as it was in days when people were less self-reliant. But I experienced the providence of God and had a very strong sense of his presence throughout the whole journey. There really were no moments when I regretted what I had chosen to do or wished it were all over.

Without the distraction of mental work, I was able to observe and reflect. It was easy to weave these into prayer or to leave them as meandering thoughts. Unhurried by deadlines, I was able to let ideas come and go. I let go of the need to make my spiritual life productive.

One of the unexpected discoveries I made was the way that a long adventure like this was so immersive. Unlike a brief holiday, the change of scene was so profound and so prolonged that I lost track of time. I spent fifty-two days largely "in the moment" and quickly developed a kind of mindfulness that let me be absorbed with wherever I was. I learned that this liberating detachment comes when we free ourselves of the burden of choice. All I had to do each day was walk to a destination. I could choose a route but beyond that, I simply had to let the walk unfold itself to me. This unforced focus led me into long periods of relaxed concentration, what the psychologist Mihály Csíkszentmihályi describes as *flow*. Paradoxically, for much of the time, I experienced the exertions of walking as effortless.

In my normal working life, like most people, I am surrounded by distractions and interruptions. So much competes for my attention that it's hard not to feel perpetually as though I might not be doing the very best thing that I could be doing. Of course, I rationalise this and work within what I feel are usually pretty reasonable priorities. But there's a quiet guilt about working in a context where there's enormous discretion and choice about what I do at any particular moment. Working from home contributes to this. Public ministry, in which the prime accountability is to God, is also especially difficult in this area. It's impossible to project neat ideas about goals and objectives onto all that a vicar does. Walking had constrained me and liberated me at the same time. The joyous freedom it brought revealed the extent of my vulnerability to the haunting of undone tasks.

The adventure was essentially an intrinsic one. Most of the things that I do are in some way investments for the future, contributions to a larger enterprise, and shared with teams and individuals. I came to understand that most of what I do is validated extrinsically - by the needs or wishes of other people, or the requirements of long-term programmes. Alone and un-employed, I shared something of the spirituality of the desert or cell. I was making progress each day, but not in the sense of production or achievement. It surprised me how little it mattered when I counted off a round number of hundreds of miles.

I learned a lot about the mental mapping that we do to make sense of where we are. I discovered the distortions that travelling at speed brings to our perception of the larger spaces in which we live. I found vast emptiness in Southern England and Northern France - in complete contradiction to the myth that we live in a largely built-over landscape.

The inequalities that I saw were shocking in a way that I hadn't expected. I would have predicted that a sabbatical trip to India or Africa would have caused me to reflect long and hard about the way that lives are lived so disproportionately. But I was led to the same reflections by walking through suburbs, city centres, housing estates and villages.

I developed a keen eye for the boundaries that mark off social space. I understood why people keep to one side of a railway track or street. Walking across these boundaries I transgressed the perimeters of territories and turfs. I saw that we are not one people. Nor do the neat classifications of socio-economic type, faith or culture properly describe the affiliations and disconnections between people. We are more tribal, more clannish than we realise.

It was good to be an alien for a while. Without status, walking in the gutters and the back-paths I found myself suspected and watched. This was a humbling that I hadn't predicted and it was refreshing as well as anxiety-provoking. I often felt that my presence was an intrusion. I didn't belong among the tower-blocks of the African-French neighbourhoods. Nor did I fit into the English village. I learned that outsiders provoke hostility not by what they do but simply by being present. It was strange to be a disturber of the peace, simply as a result of walking through a district.

I enjoyed the solitude, but I also came to realise how much I enjoy people. The best hours of my walk weren't spent in the quiet isolation of beautiful countryside but in the precious social space of markets, street corners, towpaths and town centres. In these vital spots, interactions between people are constantly negotiated. I was fascinated by the way that adolescents and old people are so adept and at home in these locations. The rest of us tend to see other people as a nuisance or obstacles to us getting to where we need to be. For drivers especially, every other car is a moving obstruction. The "joys of the open road", like the "beauty of the unspoilt countryside" are codes for privacy. They are the aspiration of the selfish parts of our character. In quiet suburban avenues and in country villages, I could tell that other people would have preferred me not to be there.

Congested streets, public benches, parks and squares were far better. My dream retirement home is not a seaside cottage nor even a suburban bungalow but a city-centre flat. Walking home to Oadby revealed how far away from home I have come and made me wonder what kind of place will be home in the future.

Home, of course, suggest more for the Christian than a building or place. In theological terms, we make our way home to God. Just like the prodigal who returned to his father and was met on the way, to trust ourselves to God is to be always home-ward bound.

Appendix One - My itinerary

Day	Destination	Miles walked
	Paris	0
1	Nanterre	8
2	Conflans-Ste-Honorine	15
3	Flins-Les-Mureaux	13
4	Mantes-La-Jolie	10
5	Vernon	20
6	Vernon	0
7	Cailly-sur-Eure	14
8	Le Vaudreuil	12
9	St-Etienne-du-Rouvray	14
10	Rouen	7
11	Rouen	0
12	Montigny	8
13	Caudebec-en-Caux	18
14	Tancarville	17
15	Le Havre	17
16	Portsmouth	5
17	Ryde	7
18	Ryde	0
19	Newport	8

20	Yarmouth	9
21	Milford on Sea	7
22	Bournemouth	15
23	Bournemouth	0
24	Bournemouth	0
25	Wimborne Minster	9
26	Blandford Forum	11
27	Sherborne	22
28	Sparkford	9
29	Glastonbury	15
30	Cheddar	13
31	Knowle West, Bristol	19
32	Knowle West, Bristol	0
33	Clifton, Bristol	9
34	Almondsbury	12
35	Thornbury	6
36	Kings Stanley	19
37	Gloucester	15
38	Tewkesbury	13
39	Tewkesbury	0
40	Uckinghall	7
41	Worcester	12
42	Stourport	11

43	Kinver	14
44	Wolverhampton	14
45	Wednesfield	7
46	Wednesfield	0
47	Walsall	9
48	Lichfield	11
49	Sutton Coldfield	9
50	Atherstone	17
51	Stoney Stanton	16
52	Oadby	12
	Total	535

Appendix Two - My gear

anti-perspirant

batteries

Berghaus IV Freeflow 50 litre rucksack

Berghaus waterproof jacket

Bible

bluetooth keyboard (linked to phone)

bull dog clips

cash

chap stick

cheque book

comb

compass

Compeed blister plasters

credit cards

dental floss

driving licence

EHIC card

elastic bands

germolene

hand sanitiser

handkerchief

ibuprofen gel

indigestion tablets

insect repellent

knife, fork and spoon set

Leatherman Micra Multi tool

light camera

light shoes

light walking trousers (two pairs)

loo roll (half)

maps

Merrell walking boots

mini-torch

mobile phone and charger

neck warmer

notebook

Opinel No.6 knife

paracetamol

passport

pencils

pens

plasters

plastic shopping bag

razors

red LED walkers back light

shampoo

shaving gel

shirts (two short sleeved, one long sleeved)

skin lotion

space blanket

sun screen

sweets

Tilley hat

tissues

toothbrush (non-electric)

toothbrush and charger

toothpaste

toothpick

travel towel

trousers (light)

trousers (waterproof overtrousers)

underwear (two pairs)

USB memory stick

walking socks (two pairs)

watch

water bladder ("Platypus hydration system")

wet wipes

whistle

Zip-lock bags

For an account of my walk as it happened, visit:

http://simonwalkshome.blogspot.com